Follow

Walking with Jesus One Week at a Time

Also by Michael K. Washington

Hope: Meditations Before, During, and After Advent

Endure: Meditations for Lent and Other Seasons of Prayer

When You Pray: Words for Searching Your Soul in Prayer

Unless otherwise indicated, scripture quotations are from the ESV® Bible (The Holy Bible, English Standard Version®), copyright © 2001 by Crossway, a publishing ministry of Good News Publishers. Used by permission. All rights reserved.

Unless otherwise indicated, scripture quotations are taken from the Holy Bible, New Living Translation, copyright ©1996, 2004, 2007, 2013, 2015 by Tyndale House Foundation. Used by permission of Tyndale House Publishers, Inc., Carol Stream, Illinois 60188. All rights reserved.

Author Photo by Jantzen Loza Photography

Copyright © 2017 by Michael Keith Washington
All rights reserved. This book or any portion thereof may not be reproduced or used in any manner whatsoever without the express written permission of the publisher except for the use of brief quotations in a book review.

ISBN: 978-0-9980507-4-4

My website: www.michaelwashington.org

Dedication

This book is for my mother, Jeryl Washington, the first person to introduce me to Jesus and the author of my first sermon about him, when as a boy I was acting all those years ago. I've often thought that a parent is a person's first and primary teacher about values, faith, and spirituality. Sometimes those teachers know the depth of their roles. Sometimes they don't. The lessons from those first and primary teachers are mixed with intention and surprise, regret and pride, joy and curiosity. I am so grateful for my mother's way of bringing me up in this faith that is mine. Her generosity in sharing all that she has—and it has not all been beautiful—steadily rises and falls into the continual making of me by God's grace. If I can maintain the best of her lessons and if I can draw truths from the hard edges of her pains, I will follow our Jesus well.

Contents

Introduction 8

Remembering Beginnings 10

Unavoidable Truth 15

Being Beloved 19

Led by the Spirit 23

With Them 27

Proclaiming the Gospel of God 31

Being Made 35

Commands 40

Gathered Cities 45

Departures & Arrivals 49

Continuing to be Healed 53

Obey Him Once, Obey Him Twice 57

Listening 61

When God Chooses You 66

Name-Calling 70

Risk It 74

Withdrawing into Silence 78

Descriptions Matter 82

Family of Origin 86

Nurturing a Desire for Darkness	90
Telling Secrets	94
Adding and Subtracting	98
Knowing Just Enough	102
Cultivating the Ability to Hear	106
Respect Your Fears	110
One Image of Freedom	115
Becoming Generous	119
When Following Looks Like Leading	123
Getting Everything You Need	127
Enriching the Meeting	132
Leaving Home	137
Dealing with John's Death	142
"I'm Here."	147
Becoming Hard or Becoming Humble	152
Starting Within	157
Love on Display	161
Faith for a Future	165
Hearing with Gentle Ears	170
Understanding Takes Time	174
Ask Different Questions	178

Tending to Your Path 182

Think of Them 187

Refusing to Read 191

Downward Aspirations 195

Disorienting Dilemmas 200

The Power and Intimacy of Praying 204

Getting Warm 208

Self-Examination 212

Contemplating Death 216

Thank You 220

Yes, You Are the One 224

Next Steps 228

Introduction

I'm trying my best to follow Jesus and that means, among other things, listening to Jesus—attending to him. In this book, I am, gently, inviting you to consider doing the same.

That said, I've thought of this book as a thread, capturing the Christ-centered ramblings between me and the One whose stories we have in the biblical biography of Mark. I began with Mark because it is the oldest gospel, and Mark proves to be a full companion for following Jesus. Originally, I wanted to pull in other gospels, but Mark had enough for this devotionally focused thread. I suggest that you read the Gospel through before and after this book. You'll notice that I don't cover every passage. I sample from Mark and in doing so I'm angling to offer one reflection for each week of the year. If you read the gospel entirely during the first week and/or the last week, you'll have something to pull you in the direction of Jesus for every week.

In general, if I couldn't offer a brief, precise, and substantial reflection, I left it for to you to search alongside others in a different format; perhaps a commentary or a longer study. Jesus was clear and I want these reflections to be clear. When I can't do justice to that goal, perhaps because of the text's unique nuances, I hope you'll read the passage for your own prayerful encounter and join others in that reading.

Let me say something about the structure of each weekly reading. You have a scriptural text, a reflection, guiding questions, a prayer, and a blessing. I also include one next step in keeping with my theme of *following* Jesus. We follow one step at a time. The text is a passage from the Gospel. The reflection is what I have to say about that passage. Guiding questions intend to offer you material to consider throughout the week, perhaps material to discuss in conversation with a trusted friend or a small circle of followers. Prayers will capture the themes of the reflection and are already engaging God (so they may not come with a title/address for the God we're already walking with). Each blessing will name something about God and/or, I hope, about you.

My aim is to offer readings that present some honest God talk. Of course, you'll evaluate that. For my part, if you come away leaning further into the Gospel; opening yourself to the possibility of Jesus' love; or experiencing the sense of having been with God, my work will be worthy. Thank you for reading.

In the season after Pentecost,
Michael

Remembering Beginnings

The beginning of the gospel of Jesus Christ, the Son of God. As it is written in Isaiah the prophet, "Behold, I send my messenger before your face, who will prepare your way, the voice of one crying in the wilderness: Prepare the way of the Lord, make his paths straight." (Mark 1:1-3, ESV)

Beginnings are often forgotten. The spiritual life in general and the Christian life in particular is a life that is subject to this stilted behavior, behavior so normal that you almost don't notice it. You don't usually notice forgetfulness. If you did, you'd be *remembering*. That means that the good news the Gospel of Mark brings is sitting near the forgettable. The good news accompanies the memory of how the Son arrived.

When I think about how the Son arrived in my life, I necessarily go to the days my home church spent at a Baptist camp in Streator, Illinois and how the movement of those retreat sessions leaned toward explanations of New Testament passages about why Jesus died. When I think of the Son's arrival, I visit the prayers and words of men and women who, before that time, talked about how Jesus saved them. I think of my mother. I think of church mothers and deacons and ministers and all their words. Their collective words frame my beginning with Jesus.

For me, those words are easier to remember than the daily acts coming from them. The words sounded the same. Turns of phrases stood out. So I remembered words or I combined what everyone seemed to be saying because their words pointed to the same reality.

It's harder to remember the moments when I witnessed my mother leading us in prayer as a family, how we acknowledged God before we ate our meals, how we went to church, how we sang before we knew deep meanings to songs, and how grace-filled it was to eat with people I'd never call believers in my young mind even though that's what they were. It's easier to lose those beginnings. They are a part of the way the Son of God came; they're forgettable.

In Mark's gospel, Jesus did not come without warning. Jesus presented himself in smaller ways and smaller forms before he revealed himself in grander ways. If you try, you'll spot the ways that God in Christ came to you before coming to you. A stranger's comment. A child's gesture. A line of poetry. In the gospel, the beginning of the story of Jesus is located in the readying work of a prophet. Well, two prophets. First, there's Isaiah, and then there's John.

The Bible says that the messenger would come before the Lord in order to make straight paths. Isaiah's ministry was to the collective people of Israel. That collected set of scriptures in Isaiah encouraged God's people in the midst of suffering, exile, and despair. The first readers were in need of God's words. They needed to know what God said about their lives at the time, and God spoke through the prophet. God spoke to affirm the people's experience of suffering on the one hand, and God spoke to affirm the love that would sustain them on the other. God didn't stop with Isaiah, however. Those holy words and refreshing pronouncements from God and for God's people didn't end with Isaiah, but carried over to this second prophet.

The biblical book bearing the name Isaiah was a collective prophetic voice. God spoke through the stories and impressions of a prophetic people. Isaiah, as a book, was a more communal project in orientation than individual ministry. When I think of Isaiah, I think of the community of Isaiah – like the community of my home church. When I think of John, however, I think the opposite. In John, God chose a quirky person, a relative of Jesus, an individual to offer continued prophesy. My pastor was a John. My mother was a John. Specific persons who were prophetic. John came in order to continue in the stream the Isaiah community flowed within. And John came preaching.

John's sermon was about preparation and creativity. Prepare the way. Create straight paths. His sermon as we have in these verses was short, though I'm sure his language and passion were immense, that they lengthened his delivery. After all, he'd have to tell his listeners what it meant to do those two things. He'd have to point to practices such as repentance and baptism. Like John's audience, God comes to you and calls you to follow a particular path.

That path is made before you recognize it because it's chiseled out of your life by people you don't always see. They're called prophets. Isaiah and John were prophets for our forebears, and we have our own prophets. They are the compelling people you tend to ignore or who you *may* ignore. Prophets are both noticeable and easily overlooked. Sometimes prophets aren't even people. Anything that readies you to meet Jesus or that prepares you for the life of walking after him is prophetic. They say, in some way, "Prepare the way. Create straight paths."

Guiding Questions

1. What do you recall about your earliest moments with Jesus?
2. Who are the prophets in your history?
3. What is God calling you to prepare for or to create?

One Next Step

Notice God's prophets. Choose a designated period of time in which to track your spiritual life – six months for instance. Revisit your "calendar" from that designated time period. Think back to who and what the prophets in your experience were. It may be helpful to create a timeline or a picture as you do this. Sketch out how those influences readied you to encounter Jesus.

Prayer

You've given me more memories than I keep. But I want to remember. Will you enable my memory to flourish? Open me to what has been between us. Open me to how you've

appeared to me so I might taste from those satisfying yesterdays. Grant me connection with all the people you've used to reach me. Help me celebrate how the good news of Jesus came and still comes.
Amen.

Blessing

You are a great giver.
May I receive all that comes from You.
May I hold all that's in the ministry of Jesus for me.

Unavoidable Truth

John appeared, baptizing in the wilderness and proclaiming a baptism of repentance for the forgiveness of sins. And all of the country of Judea and all Jerusalem were going out to him and were being baptized by him in the river Jordan, confessing their sins. Now John was clothed with camel's hair and wore a leather belt around his waist and ate locusts and wild honey. And he preached, saying, "After me comes he who is mightier than I, the strap of whose sandals I am not worthy to stoop down and untie. I have baptized you with water, but he will baptize you with the Holy Spirit." (Mark 1:4-8, ESV)

John appeared. He was real. His name and testimony opens this terse, rugged account of Jesus' story. And, people hardly mention him, barely think of him. I think this is a theological error that's motivated by a sincere desire to accept Jesus. After all, Jesus is the person whom John preached about. Jesus, not John, is the main character. Jesus sits at the center. Wouldn't a focus on John be a distraction? Paying too much attention to John might lead you astray, right? I think paying no attention to John might lead to a misunderstanding of Jesus.

There's a sense in which Jesus does not come to any person, you included, without John. John may be different for each person, but there is a John lurking around the corners of every Christian's experience of

Jesus. When you look, John appears. Or, John will have already appeared. John will be doing his thing, baptizing and proclaiming. John will be in a corner of your soul muttering profound truths about you growing and forgiving and loving. John is there, as we learned from the previous passage, to lift-up how straight paths lead to the Son.

Looking into the passage, I can't help but think that Mark exaggerates his description of "all of the country" and "all Jerusalem" going to hear this baptizing forerunner. I mean, what preacher is that popular? Of course, I might squiggle away too soon. Lean into that for a moment. Consider what it would take for a country to go and listen, for people to be so spoken to that they would travel out to John to be baptized and to confess their sins. Now, this isn't church attendance as we have it in our time. This was a revival in the spirit of the Great Awakening in the United States. This was a revival in the spirit of Pentecost in the book of Acts. People went to hear John; they went in response to a moment in their souls.

Why did they go? What could he have said? They went because what he said made *soul sense*. The people—however many of them there were—traveled out to that deserted place because the words John spoke emerged from a knowing that wasn't found in the steady words of their spiritual teachers. John's words were truthful in the surprising way only prophets' words could be. He was saying something others weren't. What made his ministry exceptional was the nearness between his words and the person to whom and about whom spoke. John preached about things that readied his listeners for the Son who was in the wings. They came to hear the truth and to hear that *The Truth* was close. Those listeners couldn't help but hear truth approaching.

"After me," John said. Jesus was, indeed, following up after John, and people heard that proximity in John's words. They sensed it the way you sense the unavoidable. It's only avoidable by effort because it's too powerful to ignore without energy, intention, and soul-will. Those people could've ignored John, but it would have been hard.

You can find a way to ignore truth, soul truth, but it takes work. You might hardly notice the Johns, but you have to work to close your ears to the truth coming from their lips. As much as the Christian experience is about focusing on the person and work of Jesus; as much as it is about the examination of yourself in view of Jesus; the Christian life is also about acknowledging that there is a John in your story. There is a John in your life readying you for an encounter with approaching, unavoidable truth.

Guiding Questions

1. What person in your life has said something you had to hear?
2. How can you regularly name the prophets in your life?
3. What does repentance look like in your life?

One Next Step

After thinking about who your John is, attend to John's message. Sit with it as you think about following Jesus. One of the meanings of repentance in the New Testament is turning toward God. It immediately implies turning away from something else to turn to God. Your John might be preaching to you about repenting of something or turning some part of your life to God. Consider John's message, whatever it is.

Prayer

Help me hear well the prophets in my world. They speak for you and, in the best way, for me. Their words bring me good. Strike my heart with sensitivity to my sins. Give me the courage to go out in faraway places to repent. Give me the endurance to turn and live a baptized life. Amen.

Blessing

What a miracle to be forgiven!
I will live a forgiven life and be increasingly free from sin.

Being Beloved

In those days Jesus came from Nazareth of Galilee and was baptized by John in the Jordan. And when he came up out of the water, immediately he saw the heavens opening and the Spirit descending on him like a dove. And a voice came from heaven, "You are my beloved Son; with you I am well pleased." (Mark 1:9-11, ESV)

John baptized Jesus. There's no reason given. Mark's story was great on action and sparse on explanation. For this particular story of Jesus, the instruction was in the shadow of the behavior. This isn't always true in Luke, Matthew, and John. In Mark, you have a murky chronological point that the baptism was "in those days." And yet this strange timestamp anchors you in what was happening.

Jesus surrendered to a ritual that others were undergoing. In other words, he wasn't the only one being baptized in those days. Indeed, he wasn't the first and he wasn't the last. Jesus joined a line of people who were going out to see the forerunner. There in the dusty distance was the prophet who had gathered a school of disciples. He was popular, preaching about the coming One. Jesus would have heard of John's fame. He would have celebrated his cousin's ministry. Others, too, would come after Jesus for baptism. I imagine that John would have grown in popularity after baptizing the person whose sandals he wasn't worthy to tie. Of course, Mark's gospel rehearses the events quickly.

After the baptism, when Jesus emerged from the Jordan, God spoke in a way that gives Christians a view of the relationship between Jesus and who you'll often hear referred to as the Father. The Spirit came like a dove. A meek and gentle bird, the dove symbolized the gentle way God landed into this pivotal event in Jesus' life. A survey of scripture would find diverse ways God's presence fell among people. There were storms, winds, whispers, and tongues of fire. Here, a dove landed or, at least, that was the metaphor that Mark used to capture the moment—a bird evoking beauty, peace, and grace. Unforced and unbidden, God came gently.

God the Father said, "You are my beloved Son; with you I am well pleased." The Father was describing a distinctive relationship between himself and Jesus. It was unique and unrepeatable, and though these words were directed to Jesus then, in a way they aren't restricted to him. They echo what Jesus' life will be about: spreading God's distinct, perfect love. Jesus will live out what it means to be beloved and to be claimed by love. He'll offer that belovedness to everyone he contacts.

Being beloved is a permanent quality—for Jesus and for you. It's unearned. Jesus didn't baptize himself. He hadn't performed a miracle. Frankly, he was doing what others were doing. He showed up. He followed the crowd. And the Father, speaking in a distinguished voice, remarked about him. Of course, Jesus had a unique relationship. He was unique but he was also, in a word, common. He was like you, which means that his being beloved was shareable. This gesture from the Father is evidence of grace, a gift that God gives to you, for you, so that you can live in response to that grace which centers on being beloved.

Hearing God's voice takes humility, and humility is clear-sightedness about who you really are. You have to see that you belong to God in order to open yourself to God's voice. That humility gives you access to the truth that you are loved no matter your behavior. You are loved, chiefly, because of Christ's behavior. It's deeply unsettling, being loved that way. It's not normal. It's not the human way to love. It's not trapped by conditions and negotiations. Being loved and blessed and spoken to by God the Father—and accepting that blessedness—requires incredible courage.

Guiding Questions

1. How has baptism or other rituals enriched your walk with Jesus?
2. When you're quiet before God, what do you hear?
3. How do you express love?

One Next Step

Ritualize your discipleship. Maybe it's something you've done before and might do again. Perhaps something came to mind as you read of Jesus' surrender to the ritual of baptism. Serving in a particular way; joining a church; visiting a support group—rituals are diverse.

Take a step toward the ritual that comes to you. In completing it or coming toward it, you are coming toward your own version of what Jesus was doing in being baptized. You are stepping toward him. It is an act of becoming more of his disciple.

Prayer

You love me.
Help me accept that love.
You want me.
Help me feel that desire.
You honor me.
Help me be humble under that gift.
You speak to me.
Help me fully appreciate what you say.
You bless me.
Help me live into that life.
Amen.

Blessing

I am beloved.
I am unique.
I'm in a distinctive, unrepeatable relationship with God.
And these are true before I *do* anything.

Led by the Spirit

> The Spirit immediately drove him out into the wilderness. And he was in the wilderness forty days, being tempted by Satan. (Mark 1:12, ESV)

The worst thing about this passage isn't that Jesus was tempted; the worst thing is that the Spirit set him up for it. God's Spirit drove Jesus from baptism to temptation, from the Jordan to the wilderness. One place echoed of God's blessing while the other resounded of the enemy's voice. The contrast reverberates. It's the Spirit that takes Jesus into the company of Satan, of the wild animals, and of the angels. He doesn't get to just spend time with angels. He's headed into his own terror.

In his experience sits a dynamic that describes spiritual leadership. Being Spirit-led means being led into certain company and into certain places, company like Satan and places like the wilderness. The Spirit had a role in baptism, but Mark lifts up the Spirit's leadership of Jesus into the wild, terrible places. Reading through chapter 1, you can almost forget that God was in those early baptismal waters. God's voice had pronounced blessing upon Jesus, a memory that likely empowers Jesus for his next experiences and inspires him through temptation. But God didn't stop at baptism. God kept speaking, drawing Jesus into darker, more dismal places. Being blessed implies this movement where the same God who lures you with blessing drives you into wildness.

    This doesn't strike me as a good plug for involving oneself in the activity of the Spirit. It's not grand or glorious, and it doesn't sound like a commercial I'd like to hear. The Spirit's activity isn't appealing here. This work of God is more sober. It's, almost, sad. God, as presented here, can be trusted to send you out to the desert to enact your faith, and this God will involve you in terrible, tempting times to make you. Oh, God speaks well of you. God blesses and claims you. That's the truth of the previous moment. The truth of this spiritual moment means that the God who identifies you as his own also puts you in places where you (and the enemies of your soul) question that very truth. Going into the wilderness is a step for questioning what you heard, what you knew, and what you believed. In fact, belonging to God brings as many questions as it does identifications with your relation to the Divine.

    You don't only hear the blessing; you hear the sending. You hear who you are and where you're going. Both come, the baptism and the wilderness. You are God's *and* you feel far from God. You are a child of God *and* you feel no confidence in that reality. Both feelings come from the Spirit's immediate involvement.

    Questions and paradoxes—not having answers to all the questions—become the material of life with Jesus. There's no good answer to why the Spirit who comes like a gentle dove will also force Jesus into a context where that gentleness will be tested. We can make up answers, but the questions become the torment that makes us see God in broader ways.

Guiding Questions

1. Where has the Spirit led you recently?
2. What would following Jesus into the wilderness mean for you?
3. How do you hear what God says to you?

One Next Step

Open yourself to what's ahead. The Spirit desires to take you places, lead you places, and turn you toward spaces that are outside your comfort zone. Open yourself that. Whisper a prayer and turn in a different direction. There will be angels there. And there may be danger too. But danger doesn't mean that you'll be hurt. If Jesus has anything to teach in this text, it may be that you'll, simply, be accompanied.

Prayer

Grant me the special ability to follow Jesus into the wild places. Bring me contentment, too. When the Spirit speaks and when the Spirit doesn't, keep my soul. Be somewhere in the temptation so I know I'm not alone. Amen.

Blessing

Every paradox holds a blessing.

I will be open to every blessing.

I will embrace every blessing.

With Them

And he was with the wild animals, and the angels were ministering to him. (Mark 1:12-13, ESV)

There is another element in this passage, one more uplifting on the surface than the Spirit luring Jesus into temptation. Perhaps the best thing—after the baptismal event with its glowing reminder of Jesus' identity—is the most terrestrial, earthy detail that Mark gives us: Jesus was with wild animals, being ministered to by angels.

Sheep and oxen. Cows and camels. Hawks and deer. Pigs and coyotes. Fish and serpents. And, angels. Now, all these animals weren't in the wilderness. Fish were likely in the Jordan, but not in the dry places! My point is in seeing animals as part of the experience of temptation. How many times have you remembered that scripture includes animals *and* humans? Angels have more space in the scripture; we remember their grand entrances. We think of Lucifer, Gabriel, Michael, and the one old preachers called Raphael. But animals? Who preaches about animals? Well, maybe the fish that swallowed Jonah. There is the occasional mention of the disciples fishing all night. Even then, the fish are secondary to the disciples who had toiled and worked and caught nothing.

In this passage, the animals take a more central place. They are with Jesus and Jesus is with them. The text carries a kind of mutuality. It's clear that Jesus is the main character of Mark's Gospel, but in this verse, Jesus shares the stage with angels and animals. The One sent from God spends time with these other beings.

I wonder what they did together, whether Jesus felt a new calm among them, whether they inspired him for the ministry he would begin. I wonder if he felt an essential residence with them that he didn't sense among the humans he was driven from in the Judean country. It's instructive that there isn't more. You get, simply, that he was *with* them.

Jesus is with beings and things that you overlook. Jesus is with beings and things that you may not esteem. And that doesn't take anything away from his company among the angels. It doesn't remove the power of his presence in your life. If it does anything, Jesus being with animals expands the meaning. Jesus being with things that you don't see means that you don't have to see it all. If you've never considered Jesus being ministered to by animals or among animals, it indicates that God can be active even if you can't spot that activity.

In my mind, I imagine Jesus sitting with animals, watching them, playing with them, being careful to respect them for the wildness in them. I imagine Jesus knowing the difference between one type of monkey and another. I think his familiarity with them heightened as the days passed. Perhaps he learned how to interact with varied species in those weeks. Perhaps he preferred land animals to birds. Or vice versa. Of course, we know none of this. All we know is that for weeks and weeks, he was with them.

Jesus being among them means that Jesus is participating in activities that you cannot see. When you discipleship looks stilted and finished, return to this text. Imagine this Jesus trafficking among the animals, playing with seagulls and goats. Perhaps it will expand you as you keep company with others in your life.

Imagine spending time with the animals in your life. Perhaps they aren't animals but they're barely mentioned people or situations. Maybe this text opens you to the possibility that there is more to spend your time on than where you generally spend it. Maybe your nourishment and your recovery can come from some barely seen direction or from some usually unacknowledged creature.

Guiding Questions

1. Are there any "wild places" in your life these days?
2. How does God reach you, come to you?
3. What does it mean to serve?

Prayer

You use so much to change me. I don't count on you using animals and angels. My vision is, sometimes, so small. I restrict you and the ways you come to me. Bust through my small views and open me to the number of available people and things you can employ to minister to me. And do the same through me. Change someone through me.

One Next Step

Go out among the animals. Visit a forest or a preserve and wander for a bit. Go to the closest zoo or one that isn't so close and find a quiet place where you can sit and observe the animals. Try not to do anything beyond seeing. Your job is to not have a job. There is no assignment beyond your being there. Don't even try to learn anything or get something out of your time. Trust that the angels will be there already. Trust that you *being there* is enough and that being there is all you have to do. You will have followed Jesus just by showing up.

Blessing

I am able to be in situations I never thought possible.

I will become comfortable in previously unfamiliar places.

I will deepen.

I will grow.

Proclaiming the Gospel of God

Now after John was arrested, Jesus came into Galilee, proclaiming the gospel of God, and saying, "The time is fulfilled, and the kingdom of God is at hand; repent and believe in the gospel." (Mark 1:14-15, ESV)

When I was growing up, there was talk about four spiritual laws and how those laws captured the gospel. The saints in my church talked about a Romans road, referring to the verses that were especially important in sharing and accepting the gospel. Often accepting the gospel meant saying a prayer where you'd ask Jesus for salvation. This was a distinctly evangelical marker of becoming a Christian. Mark's words, however, have Jesus sharing something else. There is no prayer on Jesus' lips. There is no list of scriptures worth reciting or repeating. There's talk of the kingdom.

Christians proclaim the gospel, and we do well to gauge that proclamation by verses such as these—certainly, not only these verses, but not without them. *Gospel* is another way of saying good news. In this case, gospel was news about the fulfillment of what Jesus and John had been speaking of: the kingdom. The kingdom—a word with a few meanings—was near. When promoting his ministry in public spaces, Jesus used this language. The kingdom was worth describing in a host of ways and he spoke about it being active and distant, close and elusive.

Fulfillment of the near-and-distant kingdom was central to Jesus' news. So was gospel.

As Mark lays it out here, the gospel is 1) the news that the time is fulfilled, 2) the claim that the kingdom of God is near, 3) the invitation to repent, and 4) the penetrating consideration of believing these. These phrases from Jesus are full. But they don't lean toward a magic utterance or a form prayer. They are descriptive of time, of God's claim, of behavior and what's behind it. The words in Mark describe a kind of repetition. This can upset you if you're used to saying prayers, even liturgical prayers as the route to embodying the good news. Rather, these words push a soul agenda about surrendering to the news that God's life has entered your life.

When the time is fulfilled, it means that things that God wanted accomplished had been accomplished. In some way worth discerning, God's kingdom came in Jesus. That means God's kingdom demands consistent rethinking and changing toward one's self and one's world. God's kingdom, says Jesus, assumes belief or unbelief. For Jesus, picking one is inherent to living.

John's arrest pushed Jesus to proclaim these matters. Like the forerunner's sermons, Jesus' gospel was urgent but couldn't be responded to once. There was regularity to hearing and accepting the proclamation of God's news. It required regular hearing. The news was worth coming to again and again. As John preached in the desert, Jesus pressed his claim throughout the region. Belief, repentance, and turning toward God's kingdom were day-to-day behaviors that shaped his listeners' lives.

It seems that these sermon points came out of John's ministry as much as Jesus' own thought. Perhaps he and his cousin shared commentaries as they outlined the important passages about God's kingdom life. Perhaps they shared notes, agreed on major interpretations of passages. Perhaps Jesus stole John's best sermon lines, lines John wouldn't preach anymore after his arrest. I mean this in an appreciative way, of course. My friends steal all my good points and I theirs!

John and Jesus preached this good news. Theirs was a gospel that required a regular examination of their listener's approach to God and others. Proclaiming the gospel and living it meant turning toward news about repentance and belief. It seems that being impacted regularly by God's news is indispensable for people interested in proclaiming God's news.

Can you see yourself under the steady light of the good news? Being under this light need not restrict you, but it may free you. To be seen under the light and witness of the gospel is to hear regularly the possibility of repentance and the power of belief. It is for you to be reminded that God's kingdom is already in the finishing stages where you're concerned. God's not late. God's not done. But, God's not beginning either. God's news is already working in you.

Guiding Questions

1. When did you first hear the gospel?

2. How might belief, repentance, and turning shape your life?
3. What areas in your life are changing because of the gospel?

One Next Step

Summarize the gospel in your own words. Do it in a sentence. Then do it in three sentences. In writing your own words, in coming to your own terms for the good news, you are claiming it, owning it. Try it. Resist the practice of relying on someone else's view of scripture and *add to* that view. Get into things by understanding the good news personally.

Prayer

There are many things I don't know about you.
I want to know you and the news about you.
I want to be changed by what I know.
The best of me wishes to repent, be different.
Enable that part of me to grow.
Nurture in me a repentant attitude.
Let it flourish so that I'm more like Jesus.
Amen.

Blessing

God's news is worth sharing.
I will share what I've heard.
I will give away my best understanding.
I will be a truth-teller.

Being Made

Passing alongside the Sea of Galilee, he saw Simon and Andrew the brother of Simon casting a net into the sea, for they were fishermen. And Jesus said to them, "Follow me, and I will make you become fishers of men." And immediately they left their nets and followed him. And going on a little farther, he saw James the son of Zebedee and John his brother, who were in their boat mending their nets. And immediately he called them, and they left their father Zebedee in the boat with the hired servants and followed him. (Mark 1:16-20, ESV)

The four gospel accounts together give a long, full description of what it means to follow Jesus. Everything is there, and I'm aware that any attempt to summarize the good news is deceptive to a degree, because there are four accounts with stories, teachings, and truths that illuminate what it is to live life with God. That said, the definition of the gospel, in this passage, is almost too plain. *Follow me*, says Jesus, *and I will make you*.

If you're paying attention to the man, his words are, at least, unsettling if they're not offensive. I can imagine those first disciples asking, "You'll make me? I'm not already finished? I'm not accomplished? After all, I fish better than you. You're a carpenter anyway. And, I'm already completed!" To those fishermen, Jesus said, "I will make you." And somehow these fishermen joined Jesus immediately, according to Mark.

We see something in Jesus' powerful and plain articulation of the good news. He uses what we'd call "fighting words"—from my childhood. Fighting words were words people just didn't say unless, of course, they wanted to start a fight! Jesus' words held their own strength. There was a confrontation under them, and that undercurrent couldn't have been pretty. This confrontation sat on the lips of Jesus, spilling out as he spoke to them and to you. Meet him as the person who is probably nothing like you've thought him to be.

Mark's Jesus told his listeners and tells you that you're not where you think you are and not who you think you are. This Jesus tells you that you've got a world to learn before you're whole. This Jesus is clear and firm about you're not yet being made.

During my first years preaching at New Community, Peter Hong, the pastor I worked alongside, told me that I had to learn how to preach there. Of course, I had learned to preach in a Black church, a congregation of thousands, and generally in settings that were larger. Coming to serve a smaller multi-ethnic church meant many changes to my style. Although, I'm a learner who loves to learn, it was unsettling to be told—even in kind ways—that I had a lot to learn. Of course, I've been enriched by being able to preach at New Community and in churches that are unlike my ecclesial upbringing. I've grown and learned. I think of those fishermen as I think about my growth and your growth.

The act of following Jesus is immediately humbling. Sometimes, you can't help feeling stuck to the core of your identity, pressed against hard questions about things you concluded long ago. You follow him and suddenly wonder if you really are good at what you've been told you're good at. You follow and question where your identity comes from and whether that location still satisfies your heart. Following Jesus makes you question. Following Jesus makes you see yourself. Following Jesus makes you see.

You see who you are and who you aren't. Jesus is all too willing to unfold these things to you, and very directly. You step into a crew, a community, or a group that reminds you of your previous steps *and* how far you have to travel. *Discontent* begins to characterize your spirit. You experience unsettledness in your heart where you once were convinced. You're suspicious of things you never thought of much less critiqued. You hear him, and in going with him, you are continuing to buy into the truth of your un-madeness.

Now, the journey isn't always lonely. These first followers brought relatives. You, too, won't travel the road after Jesus alone. In one way or another you will be accompanied, but you will change. You will be made.

Guiding Questions

1. What are the places of growth in your life that will only emerge when you change?
2. How does Jesus change people?

3. Who is God making you to be?

One Next Step

Invite someone to join you in following Jesus. This person doesn't have to be a Christian, only someone who can join you in your following. The idea isn't to convert someone. The idea is to engage in your own conversion. Choose a person who you trust to stick with you, a good companion. Prayerfully consider how to approach them. Once you're ready, talk with them about how you're currently following Jesus and how you see yourself in the future responding to Jesus. Your definition of the gospel from the previous week may come up in the conversation. See if they can commit to walking with you, joining you, as you follow. It'd be good to talk together about what that means and how that looks. It's not about their conversion. It's about yours.

Prayer

I know you love me as I am. I also know that you won't leave me unchanged. Somehow being different is a way of gauging how close I am to you. I'll resist, you know that. But don't leave me. I'll fight to manifest all the goodness you've placed in me. But don't give up on me. I want to be who you've made me. I want to be whole.

Blessing

I am made for greatness.
I am made for love.
I am made for peace.
I am made to build people and communities.
I am made to bring grace to the world.
I am made, by God's help, to be amazing.

Commands

And they went into Capernaum, and immediately on the Sabbath he entered the synagogue and was teaching. And they were astonished at his teaching, for he taught them as one who had authority, and not as the scribes. And immediately there was in their synagogue a man with an unclean spirit. And he cried out, "What have you to do with us, Jesus of Nazareth? Have you come to destroy us? I know who you are—the Holy One of God." But Jesus rebuked him, saying, "Be silent, and come out of him!" And the unclean spirit, convulsing him and crying out with a loud voice, came out of him. And they were all amazed, so that they questioned among themselves, saying, "What is this? A new teaching with authority! He commands even the unclean spirits, and they obey him." (Mark 1:21-27, ESV)

We don't have a lot of curricular content in Mark's gospel, but we do have clues that Jesus took seriously the role of teacher. Indeed, Jesus teaches almost as much as he does anything, even if he teaches implicitly.

Capernaum being his home base, Jesus went to the synagogue, and his rabbinical skill was praised by his listeners. You can't read the gospel without sensing the skill and impact of Jesus' teaching. And still, he was within his Jewish tradition as a teacher and learner. He spoke with power but he was well within his religious limits if that makes sense. Jewish rabbis taught all the time. What separated Jesus was not his teaching.

Indeed, there were people in the synagogue that needed more than teaching, and when they saw Jesus, they couldn't help but cry out from their pain. Before going to that part of the scripture, notice that Mark uses *immediately* often. This word misleads. When it comes to God, little happens immediately. If you believe Jesus will respond immediately or that you'll immediately and always be where Jesus is, pause. The man in the text was "immediately there in their synagogue," but that's not true for you. You're not immediately surrounded by Jesus and you're not always astonished at the man with authority. In other words, what was true for this man probably isn't true for you. Immediately may not be your word. Mark's use of the word is inspiring but I challenge you to experiment with other words in its place. Perhaps there are words or phrases that better reflect your experience with Jesus. Slowly. Years later. After three miscarriages. When I couldn't pray again. Ten years after the divorce. Find the fit.

When the unnamed person in the text arrived in the synagogue, he knew what others would learn later—that Jesus was the Holy One of God. I think that this acknowledgement is the most important part of Mark's passage. It isn't that Jesus was a teacher. This is something we'll learn in many places. It isn't even that the people found Jesus compelling. Again, that comes through other verses. What's unique to this set of verses is the man with an unclean spirit speaking an exceptional truth that only Jesus could appreciate. Jesus was the Holy One of God.

It's an exacting way that Mark, through the utterance of this man, describes Jesus. With echoes of a first testament title for God, i.e., the Holy One of Israel, Jesus is ascribed a worth that's fit for God. He is the Holy One. His authority extends beyond the lines of others in the grandest way. He is set apart, unparalleled. What he says matters differently.

The man's acknowledgement was so exceptional that everyone else downgraded it in preference for instruction. They complimented Jesus' teaching, made reference to his authority, and compared him to scribes who didn't speak with the instinctual conviction Jesus did. They downgraded truth because it hadn't occurred to them. They couldn't quite take in what the man said. Have you ever done that? Have you ever critiqued what you couldn't understand? Perhaps you couldn't accept what someone of a different race said about life. Perhaps you couldn't empathize with an agnostic co-worker.

In all this, Jesus silenced the man because the truth claim was known only to the two of them. What the delivered man knew about Jesus could be shared, but it couldn't be understood. It couldn't be accepted, embraced, and appreciated. Perhaps there is an exceptional truth that you know about Jesus. Quiet your soul for a bit and see what emerges in the quiet. Perhaps you can call him what this man does, the Holy One of God. If you can, you understand something beautiful about being a follower of Jesus. If you don't, wait a while and try again tomorrow.

Guiding Questions

1. What words would you use in place of *immediately*?
2. How do you find Jesus exercising authority in your life?
3. What do you notice stirring in your soul after sitting with this passage?

One Next Step

One of the more maturing behaviors of followers is the ability to admit limits. Consider yours. They are the things you know you can't do. They're what you've been told about yourself by others. You've heard about these limits many times. You have trouble accepting them. Go through the week thinking over the blessing of limits. As they come to mind or as you meet a limit face to face, admit it into your heart. As you take it in, name it as a limit and a gift. It may be a way to recognize something about yourself and your God.

Prayer

You are more than I understand.
You are beyond my best conceptions.
You are wider in your invitation than my hands can hold.
You are wider than my mind can grasp.
Open me to that reality.

Humble me so that I'm able to see, hear, and sense you.
Deliver me from every evil.
Amen.

Blessing

Because Jesus is more than I can imagine, my imagination can be a canvas on which God grows me. I will be open to images of God that extend me, stretch me, and grow me.

Gathered Cities

And at once his fame spread everywhere throughout all the surrounding region of Galilee. And immediately he left the synagogue and entered the house of Simon and Andrew, with James and John. Now Simon's mother-in-law lay ill with a fever, and immediately they told him about her. And he came and took her by the hand and lifted her up, and the fever left her, and she began to serve them. That evening at sundown they brought to him all who were sick or oppressed by demons. And the whole city was gathered together at the door. And he healed many who were sick with various diseases, and cast out many demons. And he would not permit the demons to speak, because they knew him. (Mark 1:28-34, ESV)

There is more healing in the ministry of Jesus than almost any other descriptive act. Healing happens throughout his public ministry, and you get the first glimpse of Mark's rendering of healing in this passage. Notice the urgency. The immediate is there again, the suddenness as the event occurs. By now in the gospel, you've seen Jesus announced by a notable and eccentric prophet. You've read of his baptism and temptation, and here the unleashing of the ministry of God's kingdom looks like healing. Healing was the picture of the kingdom.

There were other elements for sure. Jesus preached and told what the kingdom was. He taught with parables and stories. He prayed in order to exemplify a deep and basic behavior. But, he enacted and enabled people to visualize God's kingdom when he healed. In other words, healing was the expression of the kingdom. It was a way to show what God was doing.

Jesus healed Simon's mother, and there was a full day before the city gathered at the door. I encourage you to consider that day, what that afternoon would have been like, and how that hospitality would have been a flourishing display of affection between the healed mother and Jesus and the others present. We don't have details. We don't know what Simon's mother said or what Jesus did. We know that they spent time together and are left to imagine the conversations that the healed mother and the healer might have had.

Jesus was becoming well-known. He was reaching out and lifting up others. Family members were being blessed and turning into servants who were whole. I imagine that Simon's mother was responding with hospitality both because she was expected to and because she was healed. It's worth it to distinguish what you do because of social obligation and what you do from gratitude. This mother, as a whole woman, made others whole. She invited others to become comfortable in her home—the home of a healed person. If healed people serve in this way, why not invite every oppressed person? If whole persons serve and welcome, let's not constrict God's kingdom work.

Are you acquainted with this aspect of Jesus' ministry? His motives are on display for the people following him and listening to him. The whole city gathered to participate, not just in the liturgy at the synagogue, but in healing. There is a strong sense that people came to participate in the miracles of Jesus. He was popular, and who doesn't like a miracle? But, think about how the city responded to the healing of this particular woman. They knew Simon's mother, likely knew of her ailment, and probably knew that if she was *really* healed, there was little else this Jesus couldn't do.

If Jesus could heal her, there were other things that were easy for him to accomplish. Let that be a comfort to you as you consider your full life. There may be difficulties, real problems, and even conditions that stop you from flourishing. Offer those things to Jesus. See what he can do. Perhaps you'll see your worship service, small group, and conversations with new vision. Perhaps they are eligible for transformation because of the presence of Jesus and the work of God's kingdom. One thing is true: those gatherings in your life would look like Jesus was present. While Jesus doesn't have to act at every meeting, he may.

Guiding Questions

1. What remains for Jesus to heal in you?
2. How are you serving at this time in your life?
3. Where can you point to examples of God's kingdom around you?

One Next Step

Take one step toward healing. Diagnose something that hurts with the help of trusted healers, people whose hands God uses to make others whole – maybe a co-worker, a friend, a therapist, a spiritual director, a physician. Or, examine a part of your soul that's been bruised because of mistreatment. Or, listen to an ache in your spirit that you know is present, but do not fully understand. Any part works. Indeed, you may have another that emerged as you read. Take one step toward healing. Just one. And, in taking that step, you'll be in step with Jesus.

Prayer

You know what happened to me. You know the things, events, and people who sickened me. You know well where I hurt. What can I look forward to given my pains? I want to be whole. Lying on the sideline feels disempowering. I'm waiting for you to visit me. I'm waiting for you to make me. I'm waiting for you to make me whole. Amen.

Blessing
I am meant to show how God's kingdom looks. I am meant to bless others, heal others, and strengthen others. I am meant to be whole.

Departures & Arrivals

And rising very early in the morning, while it was still dark, he departed and went out to a desolate place, and there he prayed. And Simon and those who were with him searched for him, and they found him and said to him, "Everyone is looking for you." And he said to them, "Let us go on to the next towns, that I may preach there also, for that is why I came out." (Mark 1:35-39, ESV)

I choose to think through this passage in a particular way, namely, with Jesus hoping for something. He seems to long, almost hunger, for something he missed in the bustle and movement of his ministry. He looks in humbler places, in desolate places, and he seems to search for some quenchable thing that was heretofore unquenched.

Activity only went so far. The language and teaching of the kingdom only contributed so much. Jesus was hungry for something other than expressing and demonstrating God's kingdom power. Jesus was possessed by something else that wasn't constrained by meaningful acts and helping others. There was more.

Rising early in the morning, during those hours when no one in their right mind *wants* to rise—he left the soon-to-be-crowded streets of his town in favor of the quieter routines out in a desolate place. While morning waited to trade places with night, Jesus went to pray. He even went, again, to desolate places—after the man he helped spread the news—against Jesus' charge, of his healing. He healed and he ministered to the people of the city. And, he left. He didn't stay where he was clearly useful. He rose and departed and to pray.

The content of his prayer, the language of it, isn't here. But you have the act of it. Preserved is that this man—miracle worker and demon chaser, beloved Son and forgiver of sin, preacher, and the One worth speaking of—prays. Not much fuss to it. In fact, his gestures toward God are nearly hidden, and one wonders how Mark can record such solitary intimacy. Still, you have it there, and this intimate act of praying is worth imitating. Leaving the important people. Departing from good work. Walking away from the convincing rooms of others who are better for your presence. Going off into the distance even though there's more to do.

He left. You aren't given what he prayed in this passage. That will come later. But perhaps his act can form or inform your next actions. Perhaps Jesus can teach you through his leaving to pray. His act may not change your motives, but it may change your behavior. Perhaps your openness to behave in a prayerful way is an opening that God can expand.

Be flexible with assuming the morning or the evening is important to mimic. Perhaps you can't rise early in the morning. Be sensitive to your desire to pray more than being aware of any excuses that might prevent you. If you notice desire emerging, desire to commune with God, it doesn't matter when you do so. It's like the content that we don't have of Jesus' prayer. It's less important. For Jesus leaving one place and going to another place was important. The going and the coming were what matters. Answer the desire that's emerging. That matters.

Leaving communities of affirmation is hard. You want to be complimented. You want to do good work. That's part of why God has you where you are, right? It is why you're there, but it's only a part of why God has you there. What's just as pivotal is the hard departures and the, sometimes, even harder arrivals. The hard departures from places where you know you're effective. The hard arrivals to desolate places where nothing seems effective. Envision grace meeting you in each movement. Be open. There may be surprises ahead.

Guiding Questions

1. Where are you and Jesus headed together?
2. What places are hard for you to leave these days?
3. How might God bless you at your next desolate place?

One Next Step

Plan a beginning. It may not be easy because it may require that you plan an exit, too. You probably have lived through beginnings, seeing the connection between what you leave and what you start. Friend, there are beginnings ahead. Take comfort in that, and prayerfully wait for the Spirit to open a way in front of you. As that way opens, as a crack widens, name the stages of your growth, articulate what you'd like to see, and claim your steps for following the Holy One. You will have planned a beginning with Jesus.

Prayer

I am not looking forward to this. You know I hate the quiet. I hate sitting still while nothing happens. I've been raised to believe that noise means effectiveness. I've bought into my identity being shaped by my productivity. I'm mostly convinced that I have to do things to be valued and valuable. Be gentle with me, but lure me into that loving silence. Bring me into the desolate quiet that holds so much. Wait for me. I'm coming. Amen.

Blessing

I will not fear the desolate places in my life.
I will not flee from them.
I will not be alone in them.
I will be accompanied no matter what.

Continuing to be Healed

And he went throughout all Galilee, preaching in their synagogues and casting out demons. And a leper came to him, imploring him, and kneeling said to him, "If you will, you can make me clean." Moved with pity, he stretched out his hand and touched him and said to him, "I will; be clean." And immediately the leprosy left him, and he was made clean. (Mark 1:40-42, ESV)

Mark's gospel focuses on the expressed ways in which God's kingdom comes. Jesus embodies the kingdom by healing. He stretches the borders of the spiritual community of the Jews by healing the man in this passage and bringing him from the outer region of the Jewish community.

As with this unnamed man, the most marginalized people found Jesus and he helped them. The man in this text had his membership with a disinherited congregation. Based upon earlier religious laws, he couldn't traffic in the company of healthy people. Considered ceremonially unclean, he had to stay away, and the line between having to stay away and feeling unwelcome is thin.

Imagine him, feeling cast away, distant from the religious community that birthed and cultivated his identity. He was left out. Remember that this was Galilee, a distinctly Jewish community. While Jews weren't the only people afflicted with leprosy, Jews were the people who observed the Levitical laws which forbade social interaction with the ill. The spiritual community maintained these laws out of deep obedience to God and devotion to God's instructions. That obedience and devotion had consequences for this particular man and others like him. He was marginalized by the community that made him. Until he was recovered from sickness, he was set outside of the borders of the people who made his identity as a person possible. In contending with his illness, he also fought with the sibling demons of alienation and sorrow. He wasn't allowed to be with his people; he lost the meaning that came with participation in religious and cultural life. Being sick had painful consequences.

Restricted to the border regions of his community, he moved out of loneliness and fear to find a healer in Jesus. He wasn't sure what Jesus would do. His uncertainty left a prayer settling at the bottom of his heart, and you can relate to it. This man didn't know how Jesus would react. You don't know how Jesus will respond to your needs. No one does. Approaching Jesus is always and at all times an approach of faith. It takes courage.

Responding to the notion that God wants you healed takes faith and courage. Believing that the famous Jesus can take away your sorrow and return you to your community takes faith and courage. And, so does walking toward him when you're expected to be on the outskirts.

Jesus willed this man's wholeness, gave him instructions, and kept moving. Full of compassion, Jesus told the man to follow the customs of their common faith. See the priest. In other words, let him affirm that you're healing according to the laws of Moses. The man's leprosy was gone, but he still needed the community. He was healed of one thing. There was more to be done. Even though he was moved by compassion, Jesus didn't accomplish every needed thing. Jesus left some therapy, some curative work to others.

Imagine the kingdom of God in this way. The kingdom includes this one-on-one activity *and* it includes others. Kingdom faith isn't private even if it's personal. It's both personal and communal. As much as he heals the man of the alienating issue, Jesus leaves room for the people to do what only community can do.

Think about how God has used others in your own restoration. It's most likely that God has never quite *done it all* (although he is quite capable). God has probably always used others in healing you. Expect it. Don't be surprised by it. Be as thankful as you can that God comes to you through the affirmation of the priest, through the words and deeds of others. God heals you and keeps healing you.

Guiding Questions

1. If you traced it, where would your doubt begin?
2. How do you define healing?
3. What are you asking God to do?

One Next Step

If you can recognize that God is not finished with you, you know what it means to wait. Still, waiting on purpose is another matter. For this next step, that's what I'm inviting you to do: to wait intentionally. I'm inviting you to wait for something by intentionally sitting with what's present. Take ten minutes and sit where you won't be distracted. There will be enough noises in you so try to be away from external noise. Simply, wait. Set an alarm for ten minutes, and do your best to wait. If your mind gets restless, bring it back when you can. Tell yourself that it will wait Say it aloud if that helps. Do it every day that you can. When you're ready, add a minute to that clock and repeat the step.

Prayer

I've walked with this for years.
I've felt alone and isolated.
I've wondered if you cared.
You heal all kinds of sickness.
Heal me of mine.
Thank you for being willing.
Thank you for your compassion.
It's felt hard to experience that from people.
I am grateful.
Amen.

Blessing

Healing surrounds me, decorates the rooms I live in.
This week, God places me in relationships of healing and not pain. I will be healed.

Obey Him Once, Obey Him Twice

And Jesus sternly charged him and sent him away at once, and said to him, "See that you say nothing to anyone, but go show yourself to the priest and offer for your cleansing what Moses commanded, for a proof to them." But he went out and began to talk freely about it, and to spread the news, so that Jesus could no longer openly enter a town, but was out in desolate places, and people were coming to him from every quarter. (Mark 1:43-45, ESV)

The twist is that this healed man disobeyed Jesus, at least, once. Jesus told him to keep his miracle quiet and he didn't. In going off to preach, he disobeyed Jesus. One can only guess if he followed the other instruction to see the priest.

Jesus took away the skin disease but left the man with clear directives. The man, undoubtedly excited, went off to preach. Was he fully healed? Not if Jesus' clear directives carried weight. On the edge of Jesus' instructions—show yourself, offer for your cleansing—were the rudimentary means of what I think of as God's completed healing. Obeying Jesus brought and would continually bring healing *if* this man followed course.

The example that we have, however, is of a man who didn't obey. He was free of sickness *and* he was disobedient. This man is an image of who participates in the community of God. Your community of faith and mine looks like women and men and children who do both. People who are healed don't always do what God says. If obedience is in step with Jesus, disobedience is a move against Jesus. People freed by Jesus in the kingdom may still choose against Jesus. This doesn't feel right to say and yet it's precisely what experience teaches. It's true about me, and it's true about you. You don't fully obey. Your efforts are partial. Your response to God may be well-intentioned and is still incomplete.

You have to wonder whether the man received all that he could have given his choices to preach about his miracle instead of following what Jesus said and following Jewish law. Don't fault him, he was thrilled, but learn from him. You see, this healed man warns you. In his behavioral sermon, if I may call it that, he warns you to stay closer to Jesus than he did. Perhaps he got something out of his sharing, but he certainly missed the opportunity for more. Following through with Jesus' words would only have brought him more than he had received already.

If you are tempted to respond to God out of your excitement for being healed, guard yourself to stay close to the words of Jesus. Guard yourself by listening over and over to what Jesus says to you. You know of people who have moved out of excitement and passion (good things) but moved away from obedience. They don't always go together. In fact, being obedient may mean being in opposition to your passions.

Who wants to go see the priest and offer what Moses commanded when your skin is clear and clean?

Here's a subtlety of following: obedience may be boring. It may be mundane or unexciting or normal. Obedience may seem unnecessary. Walking by the words of Jesus may not win you any popularity contests. Indeed, the historical record suggests the opposite. Walking with Jesus may lead to your suffering and, in some way, even your death. Jesus still says what he says.

Following his instructions may be less exciting than following your feelings. Surely more people can come to know the One who heals if you waste no time and tell them! Or maybe there's a deeper, more sustaining possibility ahead of you. Maybe you gain a new security by doing what Jesus told you to do.

Guiding Questions

1. Have you disobeyed Jesus before? How?
2. Where do you find your feelings conflicting with God's words?
3. What have you been healed from in the past?

One Next Step

When you have a quiet moment, look over your recent decisions for choices you've made that were disobedient to God, contrary to the way of Jesus. Pick from those choices, selecting a choice that you'll probably have to make again, i.e., one you'll revisit. Ask the Holy Spirit to empower you to choose differently when that choice, or a choice like it, returns. Follow Jesus in that next choice.

Follow him by first covering that future in prayer and when it returns, by trusting God for the strength to obey.

Prayer

I make excuses, good ones usually.
But they fall apart when I sit with your words.
Help me to stay with your words.
Help me to hold to your expectations tightly.
I don't want to be convinced that I'm right.
The best of me wants to believe you completely.
Increase the best of me.
Amen.

Blessing

Showing my history with Jesus brings him praise from others.

Obeying Jesus brings him delight with me.

I want to pursue his delight today.

I will be God's delight.

Listening

And when he returned to Capernaum after some days, it was reported that he was at home. And many were gathered together, so that there was no more room, not even at the door. And he was preaching the word to them. And they came, bringing to him a paralytic carried by four men. And when they could not get near him because of the crowd, they removed the roof above him, and when they had made an opening, they let down the bed on which the paralytic lay. And when Jesus saw their faith, he said to the paralytic, "My son, your sins are forgiven." Now some of the scribes were sitting there, questioning in their hearts, "Why does this man speak like that? He is blaspheming! Who can forgive sins but God alone?" And immediately Jesus, perceiving in his spirit that they thus questioned within themselves, said to them, "Why do you question these things in your hearts? Which is easier to say to the paralytic, 'Your sins are forgiven,' or to say, 'Rise, take up your bed and walk'? But that you may know that the Son of Man has authority on earth to forgive sins"—he said to the paralytic—"I say to you, rise, pick up your bed, and go home." And he rose and immediately picked up his bed and went out before them all, so that they were all amazed and glorified God, saying, "We never saw anything like this!" (Mark 2:1-12, ESV)

Six years ago, I almost missed the flight the morning I met one of my spiritual heroes. It's a long story that ends in my walking up to Rev. Gardner Taylor's home in Raleigh, NC to interview him with Marshall Shelley for *Leadership*. We spent just under three hours with Dr. Taylor, and I was thrilled as I wrote notes on the plane that afternoon, capturing a quasi-verbatim, clenching the turns of phrases from the poetic pulpit exemplar. Remembering was its own reward. Marshall recorded the interview and had it transcribed. When I received the audio files and paired them with my notes, they became an added bonus. They were gifts because more was there than could be in the printed interview. They were ways for me to recall what the moment was.

I think that interview when I come to this passage. I'd love to have been in the audience, in the room, in the crowd, jammed in the corner to hear Jesus. I'd eat up his inflection, sit and take him in as completely as I could. I'd wonder what all the excitement was about when the paralytic got up and went about his day. I'd be stuck at some turn of phrase, some fitting metaphor, some superb analogy. And then, I wonder if that's really true about me in my imagination. I wonder if I'd hardly be moved, be barely persuaded, or sit oblivious to his words, waiting for a miracle to thrill me rather than his words. Would I forget? The folks in Jesus' audience zeroed in on a miracle and a comment as he was preaching the word to them. It doesn't make the ministry of preaching sound great. There was so much in whatever Jesus said. He's Jesus! But people seemed to focus, as Mark lays it down, on the controversy during the man's healing.

Now, to be fair, I'm a pastor. I've been to schools to learn about being a pastor. So I have opinions about what people say when they're preaching. I *feel* the scribes in this passage. I can identify with wanting to make sure this man's interpretations were solid. I know what it means to caringly answer people's questions after a bad sermon by a visiting minister. When it came to his audience, Jesus wasn't dismissive. He was patient. He engaged them. He asked them good questions to address their theological matters and he pushed them intellectually until they couldn't question further. Both were gestures of respect.

Think about it. You know what it's like to have full conversations with friends, words that need unpacking. I wonder if most of Jesus' messages were that way, if that's why we're still turning ourselves to his words after centuries. Indeed, even people who don't follow his teachings read him. They do this because the life springing from his words is endless and enduring. What he says feels soul-tested and still I find myself looking for the next exciting thing. What about you?

Following him seems to always include the confrontations, the arguments, and the miracles. Those moments are charged! I pray that the words that Jesus says can do something similar inside you, that his words can lift you the way his miracles often lifted people. I don't think his miracles were pointless by any means. I see them displays of his message; you need both.

Guiding Questions

1. Who are your favorite teachers, preachers, or speakers?
2. Is there a particular saying of Jesus that you keep close?
3. How would you characterize Jesus' ministry in your own words?

One Next Step

Sit with this biblical text again and turn your ear (or your inner ear) to what Jesus is saying to you now. If you are especially hopeful that God will do something in your life, that God will act in a particular way, listening to Jesus' words may be a challenge. You may need God to work, to act, or to do. Sit with Jesus' words and stretch yourself to hear him even when you may most need him to act. If this step feels approachable, look into the practice of *Lectio Divina* as an additional next step.

Prayer

Search me and see me.
Examine my heart for my questions.
Deal with my interests, needs, and loyalties.
Teach me how to see what matters.
Show me what I need to see.
Banish my blinders gently.
Help me pay attention.
Amen.

Blessing

My questions can lead me to Jesus.
I will use my questions to get closer to him.

When God Chooses You

He went out again beside the sea, and all the crowd was coming to him, and he was teaching them. And as he passed by, he saw Levi the son of Alphaeus sitting at the tax booth, and he said to him, "Follow me." And he rose and followed him. (Mark 2:13-15, ESV)

Usually when I read Jesus' words, he doesn't strike me as offensive. I mean he's striking, remarkable, even memorable, but this passage brings out the relationship between following him and accepting who you really are.

Levi was a tax collector which meant he was a Jew who started working for the government in order to take taxes from other Jews. His role as a Jew who collected taxes meant that he also enriched himself in the process. He took more money than the government needed and he kept it for himself. He was regarded by the Jewish community as a traitor. He was a cheat. Mark tells us that he was among those following and more importantly, he was among those Jesus called.

In inviting Levi to follow, Jesus turned the idea of rabbis taking students upside-down. In calling Levi, Jesus showed that he'd take anybody. It's both inclusive and repulsive. Jesus was indiscriminate in his invitation. Think about that. He'd take anybody. He was, in this considered motion, ultimately inclusive. He took Levi and in taking Levi, you see just how preposterous this man's ministry was in his social context. As a rabbi, he took as students the scoundrels of his day, the traitors to his race, the people, if he were sane, he wouldn't be able to stomach. In his own day, Jesus took the worst of the worst. That's wonderful for those who fit the category of worst. What about for the other religiously faithful Jews? What about people with more discriminating tastes?

Some people can't quite accept that Jesus really takes anybody. It's hard, very hard. But it's a leveling dynamic that must be true in order for Jesus to take any of us. In other words, for Jesus to take anyone, Jesus has to take everyone. His call is open because his kingdom is open. He includes as students (who will be disciples and who will become leaders) those who Jewish society said weren't respectable. This is really hard to take when you have standards that are higher than God's. Perhaps it's best to try to be *like* God when that impulse to exclude leans us toward trying to be God.

The longer you walk with him, the more you hear Jesus calling everybody. Beyond that, you realize that everybody he calls is a sinner. Not just Levi but you. You're sick, too, because of sin. That's your inescapable predicament. There's more to you, for sure. You are more than sinner, but the word sticks out from your soul like an abandoned flagpole at a shuttered neighborhood school. It's there, standing out, identifying what once was and what still is. You are both. So name your sins and claim your calling. They come from the mouth of the same Jesus. He wanted a Jewish tax collector, in part, to communicate that no person was unreachable by the social expectations in God's kingdom. Remind yourself that Jesus knew of Levi's background and he knew yours.

It may be a stretch to say that Jesus called Levi because of his background—because he was a tax collector. Maybe Levi was converted. Maybe he wanted something different. Maybe Jesus' call came out of a combination of things. Nonetheless, that man with his background sin was the person God chose.

God chooses you and knows what comes with that choice. You'll have enough opportunities to question your call from, and use for, God from the enemies of your soul. Don't add to their list. Tell yourself what Jesus told Levi. Let the enemies and demons say what they will. Let these words from Jesus echo in your spirit: Follow me.

Guiding Questions

1. What do you struggle with from your past?
2. How do you listen to the truth about yourself?
3. When is it easy/difficult to believe that God chose you?

One Next Step

As a show of faith—and a show of following Jesus—think about a way that you can express acceptance of a person you're currently struggling to accept. Imagine the person as acceptable to Jesus, as called by Jesus. Open yourself to one way that you can express consistency with Jesus. Perhaps you can say something positive that you wouldn't ordinarily say. Perhaps you can give the person a consideration that you've not yet been able to. Whatever it is, think of the person as eligible for Jesus' community and therefore, as eligible for better relationship to you.

Prayer

Have you seen what I've done?
Are you sure about wanting me?
There are so many more qualified people.
I'm not the most moral person.
Why would you want me?
Why would you call me?
Do you know what you're getting with me?
I can't see what you see.
I see my yesterdays.
Show me what you see.
Help me see.
Amen.

Blessing

I am a sinner and I am so much more.
I will allow my sins to acquaint me with humility.
And I will humbly follow this great Savior.

Name-Calling

And as he reclined at table in his house, many tax collectors and sinners were reclining with Jesus and his disciples, for there were many who followed him. And the scribes of the Pharisees, when they saw that he was eating with sinners and tax collectors, said to his disciples, "Why does he eat with tax collectors and sinners?" And when Jesus heard it, he said to them, "Those who are well have no need of a physician, but those who are sick. I came not to call the righteous, but sinners." (Mark 2:16-17, ESV)

Because Jesus was a masterful teacher, learning from him eventually opens you to learning from yourself. His teaching method moved back and forth between his kingdom and those he invited into it. He taught and embodied his values and turned those teachings and values to his followers. Seeing his values, then, turns you to seeing your own, and you naturally question, in your own way, critically wondering if what was important to Jesus is important to you. Learning from him and seeing his values involves you in a deepening examination of your own vales. In other words, seeing how Jesus taught and lived opens you to an emerging interior question: what about me?

This text comes after Jesus called Levi. He had begun to invite people like Levi to join his movement. He also invited the other disciples to become his friends. I think of that gesture, including everybody else, as Jesus including larger categories of people once he called the tax collector. His ministry and his student body, if rabbis had them, would include people like the people Jesus was calling. Tax collectors and sinners were the logical assemblies extending beyond Levi because his circles included people like himself. If he was eligible to join Jesus, his friends and associates would be, too.

What an image of who Jesus calls! Now, he didn't only call tax collectors. You'll notice fishermen were among his disciples. There are also people following Jesus whose work we know nothing about. It's helpful to remember that Jesus invited people whose work was common (i.e., fishermen), whose work was hated (i.e., tax collectors), and whose work was unknown (and perhaps unimportant as a detail). Work mattered but it wasn't a primary means to a person becoming eligible to be with Jesus.

When you think about your way of being in the world, think about who is with you. Jesus' choice of these folks shows his values. You see his way of being. Starting from the bottommost place in his society with those most despised, he brings that bottom up by graciously including them as his disciples. He eats with sinners. He talks theology with scholars. Eventually he speaks with the Roman governor. His reach covers everyone, and he's increasingly inclusive in his effort to embody what the kingdom is.

I love that we don't hear Jesus labeling his acquaintances and friends. We hear him quoting his questioners but not himself labeling people. There is something in that for you. Perhaps Jesus can teach you how to expand or restrict your name-calling. Levi is Levi, a man with a name. Jesus probably doesn't go around calling Levi by other people's labels. "Hey, tax collector." "You, the one nobody likes." "Traitor to your race, come here."

Rather than that, Jesus addressed the person, the named one. Knowing Levi's history, Jesus chose the powerful act of calling him what most didn't: a name. No conflict and no specific relationship to what he was. I sense that Jesus was the same way with these other "sinners," because they, too, were people with names.

He spent time with these folks. Why did he do this? That was the question the Pharisees posed. Jesus had his answer. May you be guided into listening to the question for yourself, and may you hear, in your own voice, your answer.

Guiding Questions

1. If you could change your name, what would it be and why?
2. How has your history defined you in the eyes of others?
3. What does this passage teach you about how to interact with others?

One Next Step

Take an inventory of your company. Notice your closest friends and gently see how close or distant you resemble the qualities of Jesus in your social relationships. Think about how you embody the strange diversity of God's kingdom complete with tax collectors and sinners from your point of view. The people who eat your meals and the acquaintances you give yourself to may be a window into how you might follow Jesus more closely this week and how you might stretch beyond your own borders.

Prayer

I've been known by my past. That's been both good and bad for me. I'm proud of some things. I'm not proud of everything. Teach me to hear you calling me by name. Show me that I'm valuable and not only for what I do. Teach me to be gracious to myself and to others. Grant me the patience to hear more than people's mistakes. Teach me to name people well. And in naming myself and others well, may I follow you. Amen.

Blessing

People like me love Jesus.
Jesus loves people like me.
Everybody, in some way, is like me.

Risk It

Again he entered the synagogue, and a man was there with a withered hand. And they watched Jesus, to see whether he would heal him on the Sabbath, so that they might accuse him. And he said to the man with the withered hand, "Come here." And he said to them, "Is it lawful on the Sabbath to do good or to do harm, to save life or to kill?" But they were silent. And he looked around at them with anger, grieved at their hardness of heart, and said to the man, "Stretch out your hand." He stretched it out, and his hand was restored. The Pharisees went out and immediately held counsel with the Herodians against him, how to destroy him. (Mark 3:1-6, ESV)

In some ways this passage is a picture of what's ahead for Jesus' entire ministry. His work is always about some other exhibition of kingdom power. He combines words with actions, miracles with messages, to show what being with God meant. This scene shows you what following Jesus brings. Being with Jesus meant transformed ears *and* hands; it meant changing the inner person *and* the body. Being with Jesus also meant taking risks with every next step.

I don't mean to suggest that life with God involves fear. You probably feel fear when you take risks. But the two aren't the same. Fear is an old, deep brain impulse to preserve your life. The body cooperates with that brain impulse to make you sense fear. Fear works to convince you in conscious and unconscious ways to survive. It's not a bad thing, though it isn't fun either. Risk is different because it is a step in the direction of the unknown. Unknowns aren't always bad. Risk, when you take it, involves faith. Now, these two are related. Risk and fear can be friends to one another, or they can be enemies. Fear can convince you not to take risks. On the other hand, fear can illuminate the possibilities ahead once risk is taken. This passage shows that being with God means feeling fear and taking risks.

As you read, some plotted against Jesus, even though he was helping. People wanted to kill him, and eventually Jesus would die. Jesus was doing a good thing, and in my imagination, he didn't see his good behavior as a risk as much as it was him enacting God's kingdom. Aside from how you do that very thing, it's worth remembering that right living and good behavior don't always benefit you immediately. Indeed, they may bring you down. There are people who hate the good you do, people who keep as their aim your destruction, even while you mend brokenness in your world. Some people want to harm those who bring wholeness.

This doesn't make sense. It's irrational. It's also not the only response goodness gets. Everybody didn't want to kill Jesus. This text says that the Herodians and Pharisees wanted to destroy him. However you exegete the text, it needs to be said that the hatred of Jesus wasn't widespread. A lot of people loved him. A lot of people love you. Not everyone wants you dead! The fact is that goodness gets you far because people want the goodness that you give.

Hatred is one natural response to Jesus. He brings too much to accept. But violence is not the only natural response. The other is worship which is crying out and telling the truth of what beauty you see in Jesus. Worship is sitting on the edge of your seat, expecting and hoping at the sight of him who purposes to heal, mend, and make life. Be encouraged that following Jesus involves taking risks to be surrounded by the consequences of your behavior. Those consequences may be deadly, or they may be the most life-giving gestures you've ever seen. Mark tells us in other places that the crowds came to hear Jesus. That was different than what you see in this text. It wasn't all bad for Jesus and it isn't for you.

Not knowing what will happen is the stuff of risk. It is the ground of faith under your feet. Will you do the work of healing? Or will you leave risks for someone else? That's your choice. One would certainly be in step with the life of Jesus. One would not. Today, what do you feel most equipped by God to do?

Guiding Questions

1. How would you describe the consequences of your following Jesus so far?
2. What does a risk look like for you these days?
3. How do you balance noticing the good and the bad coming from your being good?

One Next Step

Take a risk in your practice of worship, namely, by doing something that's consistent with your faith but that you've never done. It could mean attending a worship gathering in a different faith community. It could look like you using another style or practice of prayer. I don't want to box you in with examples. Consider what worship is and how you might deepen your love for Jesus by adding to that worship.

Prayer

I want to pray for those who've risked more than me. I know that they've risked and won. I know that they've risked and lost. Give them every needed thing for their courage. Bless them with the sounds of your voice when they give. Beat back fear and swell within them hope and strength. Help me take cues from them, be taught by them. And in my taking cues from them may I come closer to you. Amen.

Blessing

Jesus goes before you, taking every risk first.
He leaves in the path pieces of courage for you to pick up for your journey.

Withdrawing into Silence

Jesus withdrew with his disciples to the sea, and a great crowd followed, from Galilee and Judea and Jerusalem and Idumea and from beyond the Jordan and from around Tyre and Sidon. When the great crowd heard all that he was doing, they came to him. And he told his disciples to have a boat ready for him because of the crowd, lest they crush him, for he had healed many, so that all who had diseases pressed around him to touch him. And whenever the unclean spirits saw him, they fell down before him and cried out, "You are the Son of God." And he strictly ordered them not to make him known. (Mark 3:7-12, ESV)

Make sure you see two behaviors in Jesus around all this important miracle-working. First, he withdrew. He served others, healed others, and preached to others, but he also took leave. You'll find evidence of this throughout the gospels. Rather than stick around, Jesus would be off in seclusion and usually praying. He worked and he withdrew.

You need to do that if you're going to follow him. Withdrawing and withdrawing for prayer will nourish you when sticking around will diminish you. Most of your day is probably spent sticking around. It looks like sticking around at work, perhaps, to continue building your resume, to keep looking like a model employee, or to maintain your lifestyle. Sometimes sticking around is necessary, right? Withdrawing is the other, strange behavior that implies loosening one's grip on a schedule or set of tasks. It's risky but it brings its own rewards. You take a break. You rest at home. You eat a meal with friends. Sometimes leaving is the only way to celebrate who you are.

Try leaving in order to sit in silence with the Father. Try pulling away—physically or not—in order to reflect upon your life with God. See what's there. See what's not.

Secondly, in this passage, not only does Jesus withdraw when crowds follow, he also orders people to keep quiet. He isn't trying to be worshiped. He doesn't need people to tell him what the demons say: You are the Son of God. Jesus knows his identity. What he needs is the prayerfulness happening when he leaves one place and travels to another. He needs the sweet communion occurring as he steps away from one village and journeys to another. I think of this as God's voice and not the voices of crowds. I think that he needs the voice sitting with him in the quiet and not the voices of those who call him the Son.

I want to be careful here because I don't intend that what Jesus does can be done perfectly by you or me. It's hard to believe you don't need the praises of people, especially because that affirmation is how God reaches you. In other words, God speaks through people. In a way that means you very much need the voices and praises of others, even if Jesus didn't. You aren't Jesus, right? People have to tell you who you are, what your relationship to the

Divine is, and how you can hold onto that important truth about yourself.

Interpret Jesus' behavior, and note the connection between you and withdrawing. This passage is not an invitation to close yourself off from that affirmation from others. It is, on the other hand, an invitation to add to your life withdrawing into holy seclusion. You need both: the words of others and the words of the Other. You need what people say and what God delivers to you in the silence. You will hear many things when people talk to you. They will speak truths and lies. They will challenge you and support you. To anchor what they say is to locate the inner wisdom of God's words in an unmediated fashion. That comes through quiet, through silence, and through withdrawing.

Guiding Questions

1. Where do you need to leave and where do you need to go?
2. What might God be saying through others to you?
3. How can you turn your ears and heart to the divine inner voice?

One Next Step

Try withdrawing, for a bit. Start small by taking a specific break in order to quietly review what's going on in your day. It can be a mini-Sabbath. Use part of your break at work to do this. Or take some time to reflect upon what's happening as you go from one place to another.

You might take a ten-minute walk and review what happened so far in the presence of God. As you get used to the idea, add to it. Build up to taking a boat out on the water like Jesus and retreating to the other side of your Galilee!

Prayer

I want to listen well. I want to hear even if that means withdrawing. Help me to have open ears so my heart can also be open. Help me to hear the best of people's words. Let me attend to criticism when there's something in it for me. Grant me the wonder of your own voice. Sensitize me to the inner wisdom that comes from you. Anchor the truth so that I don't miss it. And in my listening, tell me what I need to keep after you. Amen.

Blessing

In me is truth, already, present, and waiting to be heard.

I will hear the voice of deep truth and I will follow.

I will stay close in my following no matter what.

Descriptions Matter

And he went up on the mountain and called to him those whom he desired, and they came to him. And he appointed twelve (whom he also named apostles) so that they might be with him and he might send them out to preach and have authority to cast out demons. He appointed the twelve: Simon (to whom he gave the name Peter); James the son of Zebedee and John the brother of James (to whom he gave the name Boanerges, that is, Sons of Thunder); Andrew, and Philip, and Bartholomew, and Matthew, and Thomas, and James the son of Alphaeus, and Thaddeus, and Simon the Canananean, and Judas Iscariot, who betrayed him. Then he went home, and the crowd gathered again, so that they could not even eat. (Mark 3:13-20, ESV)

Jesus went up to a mountain, a distinctly rabbinical behavior. Rabbis would find a place on the mountain and teach those who gathered near them. When the teacher called a potential student to him, that person would come, hear, and make a critical decision. The person would continue to listen and continue to follow or the person would, unable to continue, depart. He or she would return to life already in motion, following God in the best way they could. But they wouldn't attach themselves to the rabbi.

In the Christian tradition, the earliest disciples created a large group out of which Jesus chose a smaller group of apostles. That larger group was complete with spiritual forebears who are important even if we don't know their names. The second group of apostles was the specific people who would lead the movement of Jesus into becoming the church. Apostles were the ones Jesus sent in order to lead the larger group so that the work continued. They were still disciples but Jesus added to their discipleship the task of leadership.

Mark describes the apostles, and these short descriptions signify qualities of the earliest leaders Jesus used to invite others into God's kingdom life. The descriptions reveal family ties and specific unforgettable behaviors. Only a few people have these characterizations, but they are enough for Mark's point to be made. Descriptions matter.

If the descriptions are histories, each brief history is a way into the heart of Jesus and who he was thinking could benefit from his message. In considering who would join the movement within Judaism and who would stay within a stream culminating in the early church, Jesus wanted people like James and Philip and Simon. There was a place for the Thomases of the world. Further, each history is a window into who the disciples could immediately reach with Jesus' message. For instance, Judas could reach the betrayers in a convincing way. They, too, were eligible for the kingdom. They, too, were included in the work of Jesus.

Like you saw earlier in Levi's case (Mark 2:12), everyone Jesus calls has a past. That past is useful in the kingdom of God because, among other things, it links the person with a particular community of people needing access to the kingdom. In your life, that access comes through you and your testimony. You bridge others to Jesus. You bring others to Jesus. By your arrival, you make Jesus and the kingdom of Jesus available to somebody. Think of it this way. Whatever most describes you, whatever characterization is truly yours, is the stable bridge that others cross in order to arrive at God loving them.

Might this be a reason for you to stay close, or close enough, to your yesterdays? This means that God will use those yesterdays. This means that the little parentheses in your story—those packed phrases that describe where you came from—matter greatly. Your life in all its detail is retrievable for holy purposes. That changes it for you, doesn't it? There is in Jesus' call to all these types of folk redemption of where they've been and who they've been. In the hands of God, all your yesterdays look redeemed, purposeful, and beautiful.

Guiding Questions

1. What's included in the parentheses of your life?
2. Where do you struggle to believe that your yesterdays are redeemable?
3. How have you witnessed Jesus working in you or through you?

One Next Step

Redeeming your past can start with reviewing it. When you feel up to it this week, take a chunk of time from your past that was particularly painful and sit with that pain in the company of Jesus. Pray as you begin by asking Jesus to shoulder those pains with you. Then, sift through one or two events or relationships that caused you pain. See if Jesus has anything to say about that pain. He'll be with you during that review. Even in thinking it over, there is redemption.

Prayer

I don't believe that you can use every part of my story. It's hard to trust that the pain can be helpful, much less good. I don't pretend to understand or even trust it all. But I want to trust, Jesus. I want to believe that when you call, it's me you want. Upset my unbelief long enough for me to begin building faith. I want to believe that I'm loved. You're the one who can make it happen. May your Spirit do its work in me. Amen.

Blessing

I will look for a long time this week at who I am. I will be unafraid to accept myself, to see myself, to love myself. I will be motivated by the God who has only accepted and loved what I see.

Family of Origin

And when his family heard it, they went out to seize him, for they were saying, "He is out of his mind." ...And his mother and his brothers came, and standing outside they sent to him and called him. And a crowd was sitting around him, and they said to him, "Your mother and your brothers are outside, seeking you." And he answered them, "Who are my mother and my brothers?" And looking about at those who sat around him, he said, "Here are my mother and my brothers! Whoever does the will of God, he is my brother and sister and mother." (Mark 3:21, 31-35, ESV)

    If my mother heard me say that she wasn't my mother, she'd find the quickest route to my face. She might offer a story about my birth, about how she watched a movie and how it was three months too early so that she had all kinds of things to say to keep me inside when I was ready to come. But she'd think better of it, and standing in my face, I think she'd let her heavy hand do its work. She'd skip by the pretty stories. "I'm your mama," her hand would say, "and you must need me to bring you back to reality."

    I don't know that Mary was like I believe my mother would be had I said something like what Jesus said. But I imagine that Jesus' words were hard for her and for his siblings. His were stretching words, snapping words.

He pulled at the fabric of what family was, yanking at seams that before then had probably been unquestioned.

Don't forget that Jesus knew things about himself that his relatives didn't. Jesus knew he was the Son of God. Sure, Mary would have Gabriel's words etched in her heart. How could she forget the visitation of an angel! But mothers forget too, especially after months of sleep deprivation, years of worrying about this son you love, and nights of wondering if what you think is true really is. Even with that, Mary, Joseph, and their other children weren't in the same spiritual place that Jesus was. As a child, the boy was talking about being about his Father's business when Joseph was sweaty from having traveled for days searching for the child. They saw things differently.

The thing to remember is that in renaming or reinterpreting family, Jesus gave a gift. The gift was in presenting a clear moment of inspecting the uninspected. It didn't come wrapped in shiny paper but it was still a gift. Jesus pushed his relatives to a question they hadn't thought of: who are we to each other?

This was a deep opportunity for this family. It was absolutely counter-cultural because the family was the immediate means of understanding one's place in the world and, with it, one's impact upon the world. Jesus lifted that up for inspection. He made his loved ones wonder. The gift was scary but it was also clarifying.

Jesus' comment made clear who his family was. Jesus had more people in his family than his family of origin saw. Like him, you have more relatives than you can acknowledge; there are relatives in your past, present, and future. They may hold signs saying things you'd never say. They may do things you'd never do. They may have more courage than you can dream of having for yourself. They may have participated in wars that make you question whether you are the same as them because you couldn't possibly act in ways consistent with them. They could be peace-keepers or healers, political leaders or reformists. You have a broad, new family when you belong to Jesus.

Sit with the expansive image of a large reunion taking place. Imagine today, sitting around you and Jesus, is an innumerable community of God-given aunts, cousins, uncles, and grandparents. They belong to you and you them. They are with you now and they wish you only good.

Guiding Questions

1. Who is in your family of origin?
2. How does Jesus expand your family?
3. What might you learn from your enlarged family this week?

One Next Step

Draw your spiritual family tree, your spiritual genogram if you're familiar with that tool. Spend time with the exercise, naming the people who you consider to be part of your spiritual family. Think about who has influenced your spiritual development, what they've done, and how you're related to them (i.e., what you say your relationship is). Place them in your family tree. Celebrate that God has given you those gifts and expressions of love. This is also a helpful exercise for families in general.

Prayer

Make me comfortable at this splendid reunion. I don't know everyone around this table. I can't remember all these relatives or certainly not all these smiles. I'm not sure we've met before. I'm not sure I want to eat everything on this table. My mouth and middle are hesitant to take in all this nourishment. It looks amazing, like a picture of the life you have for me. Ease me so that I can enjoy this feast. Make it so that I walk away full of love, full of good memories. Make it so that in my leaving I take all of this with me. Help me remember that I belong. Amen.

Blessing

I am related to greatness.

I come from strength.

I originated in love.

Nurturing a Desire for Darkness

Again he began to teach beside the sea. And a very large crowd gathered about him, so that he got into a boat and sat in it on the sea, and the whole crowd was beside the sea on the land. And he was teaching them many things in parables, and in his teaching he said to them: "Listen! A sower went out to sow. And as he sowed, some seed fell along the path, and the birds came and devoured it. Other seed fell on rocky ground, where it did not have much soil, and immediately it sprang up, since it had no depth of soil. And when the sun rose it was scorched, and since it had no root, it withered away. Other seed fell among thorns, and the thorns grew up and choked it, and it yielded no grain. And other seeds fell into good soil and produced grain, growing up and increasing and yielding thirtyfold and sixtyfold and a hundredfold." And he said, "He who has ears to hear, let him hear." (Mark 4:1-9, ESV)

Growth is not like a menu item in a restaurant. Restaurants have ingredients. Chefs have purchased items in advance of their first reservations. Line cooks prep vegetables and refrigerate some items, marinate others. Based on the menu, cooks already know what they'll prepare even if they don't know how much on a particular night. They work together to plan a process in advance of their customers. Growth is different because you don't know what will come or when it will emerge. When it comes to spiritual growth, you don't know what God will do. There's no preset menu for growth.

The part of your spiritual life that you can control is known as your spiritual discipline. You can't control your growth but you can control your approach to it. You choose your discipline; you choose how you come at the practice of faith. That's all you. So what can you do to construct your spiritual yield? The answer is in the discipline.

You can build a frame for God to work in or you can leave your life subject to what the day brings. The day will bring sunshine where the divine seeds will burn having been overexposed. The day will light the areas of your soul seeds that need time, darkness, and long days. The day will bring rocks atop your soul seedling when you need to be shielded from heaviness. The day will bring many things.

In the language of this passage, seeing what the day will bring is akin to the sower throwing seeds in places of no depth and eventually exposing the seeds to the scorching light. When it comes to those places where your soul seeds are placed, spiritual growth never happens without darkness. It's dark work, and when there is too much light, there's little room for the spirit to move through the natural process. Darkness is an indispensable part of the process. In terms of spirituality, what happens in that darkness is a part of the mystery. You may name some of it, get at it in parts, but the wonder of it involves your inability to fairly state and explicate what's going on.

The One who knows what happens in the dark is Mystery. The One who knows what's going on is the One who has instituted the need for this darkness. In Jesus' time, his listeners knew that everything that grew needed darkness to thrive. There was no hydroculture. There was soil and sun. There was darkness and mystery.

There is an alternative for the sower. The alternative is in building a discipline to preserve what's happening. Instead of seeing what comes, the sower was to build something to preserve the good seeds planted. How does this relate to you? It means to approach your life by abandoning daily the belief that you can order what comes like a menu item. It means that you can build a discipline to house the development occurring within. You can cultivate the plant of your spiritual growth, tend to it, give it darkness, and get in dirt. That might look like prayer. It certainly includes doing what you're doing in reading this book, using these prayers, and coming to your answers to the guiding questions. In talking over these meditations with Jesus or a spiritual friend, you are building what God will use to protect your soul from premature exposure. Keep at it. Build what you can. Then, celebrate what God does from there.

Guiding Questions

1. Based upon life so far, what does dirt and dark look like for you?
2. When are you tempted to order spiritual growth like a menu item?

3. How can you embrace mystery in your life?

One Next Step

Identify the places where you feel misunderstood by God. In other words, consider your dark places, places where you know God is working but you don't know how? Name those places. Describe them so you're aware of their presence and detail. Then, approach the soul work of praying about those places. Talk and listen to God about each one. Perhaps there is a way that Mystery will speak.

Prayer

I grew up getting cleansed of dirt.
You'll understand my hesitation to sit my soul seeds in it.
Please show my fears glimpses of my future.
When the dark settles over me, tend to me.
When I get tempted to jump up and out, ease me.
When I'd rather be in the light, convince me.
When the future feels far away, show me.
When I forget the value of waiting, remember for me.
Amen.

Blessing

Darkness brings splendid things.
I will sit in the dark mystery.
I will nurture the time of quiet darkness.
I will surrender to those things growing.

Telling Secrets

And when he was alone, those around him with the twelve asked him about the parables. And he said to them, "To you has been given the secret of the kingdom of God, but for those outside everything is in parables, so that "they may indeed see but not perceive, and may indeed hear but not understand, lest they should turn and be forgiven." (Mark 4:10-12, ESV)

One way of listening to this text is hearing that you've been given a secret, a great one. Having been told a secret, you, in turn, act like a special person, grateful that you're let in on this wonderful parabolic kingdom. After all, it's true that you're special. When you've heard a truth about yourself, it is a deeply satisfying gift. Like anything precious, the truth is worth protecting, cherishing, polishing. There are things you have, answers you possess, clarity and discernment which sit down at the bottom of your being.

Another way of listening to these words is in asking how you can give what you've been given. The entirety of the Christian faith is about receiving and giving. Throughout centuries, the faith has been handed from one generation to the next because people have been generous. Storytellers shared their memories. Scholars worked hard over languages we've lost. Editors and readers worked together to ensure that what was said was also captured in written form. Preachers and teachers stayed faithful. God stayed faithful.

And you've received the fruit of all that faithfulness. You hear and tell, get and give. The message, collected in dusty pages, has been passed down, translated in languages you'd never recall, and breathed upon in each generation by the Spirit. The Spirit keeps nothing from you, and there is an ever-unfolding quality to God's work: the Spirit keeps telling you God's best secrets. The way those secrets get passed down is through the generous story-telling of saints throughout the ages. I'm convinced in this rendering of the passage.

Listening to Jesus' words means constantly peering into how you can do what's always been done, namely passing on the secrets. It's the opposite of a secret really. It's the secret that's meant to be given, the secret you only heard because someone *didn't* keep it. The inner witness of that divine spark in all humanity underlines the secret. Persons come along and say things that sound like this secret. It "makes sense" to you. And you turn toward it. You conform to what you heard. You are forgiven. You follow Jesus.

In following, you regularly come closer to doing the things that Jesus himself did. He preached, so you preach, even if you'd never call yourself a preacher. You share your testimony. You tell your story about what Jesus has meant. It's a soft way to preach! You're actually sharing the secret. Look for, notice, and live into moments when you get to do that. Share your most precious gifts. God grant that you might be generous, enabling you to hold your gifts with gentle hands, and readying you with excitement that keeps spreading.

A final point is about prayer. Jesus says that everyone can't accept the parables. Everyone can't perceive these teachings. I once heard a preacher say that no one knew who could accept the truth about Jesus and that was the reason everyone had to preach truth with passion, clarity, and zeal. Friend, if you have heard the secret, perhaps you can pray for people who need the truth of God's love. Perhaps you can support a person's turning to God by asking God to "let them in on the secret." Perhaps God will answer your prayers and that person will be able to perceive the parable, be able to understand the secret, and be able to open themselves to being forgiven and living in that love.

Think about what you've been forgiven from and forgiven for. Doesn't it turn an invisible engine in your heart? Recognize that those same sins that God in Christ forgave in you are worth others experiencing. If there is a secret in the kingdom of God—a secret about God who forgives—it is definitely not worth keeping. It's worth giving away!

Guiding Questions

1. How do you describe the secret of God's love?
2. What don't you understand about Jesus and his kingdom?
3. How can your questions about the kingdom of Jesus become prayers this week?

One Next Step

Write a prayer for someone who you know doesn't have the spiritual fortitude they need right now. It can be a person you know or a person you only know through someone else. This particular step is less about what's included in your prayer and more about the specific gesture of praying beyond yourself. In your own words, ask God to reveal a secret thing to someone else.

Prayer

I am so thankful to understand what I do about your love. Would you prepare the hearts and ears of people who need your secret? Ready them the way you readied me. Prepare them to hear, listen, and understand. You love them and they should know that love. Let nothing stand in the way of their getting that secret. Make it so that I'm useful to that person's understanding. Love and serve them through me. Amen.

Blessing

I am equipped to share.
I am capable of telling the truth.
I am well-suited for introducing others to love.

Adding and Subtracting

And he said to them, "Is a lamp brought in to be put under a basket, or under a bed, and not on a stand? For nothing is hidden except to be made manifest; nor is anything secret except to come to light. If anyone has ears to hear, let him hear." And he said to them, "Pay attention to what you hear: with the measure you use, it will be measured to you, and still more will be added to you. For to the one who has, more will be given, and from the one who has not, even what he has will be taken away." (Mark 4:21-25, ESV)

  Illumination comes to mind when I sit with this passage. Jesus mentions a particular tool of illumination, namely a lamp in its proper place. He talks about manifestation and hidden things being revealed. He encourages you to pay attention to what you hear. I think Jesus is pointing to the special way illumination comes when we use things properly. Of course, a person's ears are for hearing. It's notable that Jesus tells you to attend to what you hear.
  There seems to be under Jesus' words clear direction about the natural way of things from his perspective. For instance, lamps bring light. They aren't meant to be upside down ovals with stands protruding inside baskets. The same goes for the impact of light on what's hidden. Light reveals. This is normal. Most people with ears hear. This is natural. When you have, you'll get

more. There are normal processes, natural occurrences, and expected outcomes.

It's worth considering, from time to time, what the outgrowths of your walk with God are. I don't mean that you should base your life with God on what you get from God, where you love God and serve the kingdom if certain things go your way. God does not have to participate with your plan. You don't have to serve only if you get what you desire. Still, to ask, "What's the good here" or "What's the fruit here?" are good questions.

It opens you to honest exploration and examination. To be honest means to be humble enough to accept what is and to resist what's unreal. Humility is accepting what's present—in you, in your situation, and in your life with God. Questions like these two that I mentioned make or keep you humble, and they help you evaluate what's actually happening. You look at yourself honestly, opening yourself to the light of God. When you ask these kinds of questions, you're doing the opposite of hiding. You sit next to that basket rather than under it. You listen as the Spirit speaks about the hidden things in you that need revealing.

Spirituality sits close to the ground in this passage. Following Jesus really means plain and pedestrian stuff like using lamps for their proper purpose, placing them where they can make the most darkness flee. There's also a response to this terrestrial, plain, and humble spirituality. I call it adding and subtracting.

In Jesus' words, "more will be added to you" or "from the one who has not, even what he has will be taken." Attending to what you hear and what you have leads to getting more. Losing a sense of what you hear and have leads to loss. Following the natural process that Jesus lays out will lead to more being added to you. The opposite is true as well. When you lose sight of who you are—when you're proud and unrealistic—you lose the little sense of self that you've cultivated.

Jesus doesn't offer a formula here, but he does offer wisdom. Wisdom is knowledge that can be put to use. Wisdom is information that can be practiced. Rather than give you a step by step view of what happens when you do this or that, Jesus offers a glimpse of knowledge in motion.

When you follow him, these are the things you can expect. When you follow him, you can expect more or less. You can expect to be pressed to hear. You can expect to gain or lose depending on what you choose. If you pay attention, you'll gain. If you don't, you'll lose.

Guiding Questions

1. What images come to mind when hear Jesus' words about paying attention to what's present?
2. How do you define humility?
3. When are you most able to pay attention?

One Next Step

Consider feedback you've heard recently, feedback that you sense has truth to it. This next step involves taking a few minutes to chart a plan for how you will pay attention to it. Write down 1) what the feedback was; 2) how you felt about it; 3) what's immediately true; and 4) what's hard to accept. Offer each one of those answers (or each set of answers) to God quietly. Then, ask yourself what's there for you to hear. You may find yourself reflecting upon or holding Jesus' words in a particular way during this next step. Good for you.

Prayer

Open my eyes so I can see what you've placed ahead.

Open my ears so I can hear what you've said.

Open my heart so I can love the people in my life.

Open my soul so I can relate to you well.

Open my hands so I can serve the world with what I have.

Open my imagination so I can keep seeing and hearing.

Thank you and amen.

Blessing

I am able to hear what God wants me to hear.
I am able to hear what I need to hear.
I am able to hear.

Knowing Just Enough

And he said, "The kingdom of God is as if a man should scatter seed on the ground. He sleeps and rises night and day, and the seed sprouts and grows; he knows not how. The earth produces by itself, first the blade, then the ear, then the full grain in the ear. But when the grain is ripe, at once he puts in the sickle, because the harvest has come." (Mark 4:26-29, ESV)

 One of the qualities to the teachings of Jesus is plainness. Though he could debate with the brilliant sages of his day, this great teacher spoke to the common person. He spoke in plain language. His teachings took the form of words that everyone could understand. When speaking to the common person, everyone could follow him. Those with basic vocabulary and those with advanced skills. Everyone started with the basics. Everyone could hear him.
 Jesus was at home discussing the scriptures with social outcasts, even while he engaged in dialogue with the socially privileged. In either case, he got responses from his audiences because they knew where Jesus was coming from. They could follow his words and his logic. Beyond that, Jesus' first listeners knew what he meant because his approach was through stories. Therefore, his intent was clear. He wanted to engage.
 Jesus approached his work masterfully and gently, employing the accessible techniques that some of his

contemporaries shunned. Why use a story when an imperative would do just fine? Why engage people's imagination if you could, simply, tell them what a saying meant? Jesus used objects that his audience could understand, engaged the imagination, and turned the souls of his listeners to God. He met their heads and their hearts.

When illuminating the kingdom of God, Jesus spoke of seeds scattered on the ground. The person scattering saw the result of his scattering but not the process behind it. Similarly, the earth produced the blade, ear, and grain, and the result was harvest. In God's realm, things have a sense and logic. In the kingdom, you can expect certain things even if you cannot explain them.

It's easiest to focus on the person in the text because you are a person. You're not the earth; you're not grain. You can identify with the person who throws seed and sees the produce of the un-earthing, digging, planting, or throwing. There is another feature to this passage, one that involves accepting the humility in not knowing how the sprouts emerge. You see, you are a person but you also are growing. You are like the crop that's planted.

God placed something in you. Something grows in you that you didn't start. I think of how God is at work in ways you can't fully know, at least, while the dirt covers you and before the sprouts emerge from the ground. If you can't fully know what God is up to, you probably can't see everything either. You're in the dark, and you are inside the workings of the kingdom at the same time.

You step inside the field of clear-thinking, sleeping and rising and accepting what God brings. As much as you can relate to the person who plants, you can also know, in a deep way, what it means to be planted. I think of this as knowing just enough. You know you're in the dark, and that's just enough. You know God placed that desire in your heart, and that knowing is just enough. When the full picture is unavailable, when the whole plan is not revealed, celebrate what you do know.

Guiding Questions

1. What are some of the gifts God has planted in you for the world?
2. How would you describe what's growing in you?
3. What do you understand about Jesus and what leaves you mystified about him?

One Next Step

This next step is an attempt to grow your waiting muscles, that is, the muscles that help you wait. When the harvest comes, it's relieves you from waiting, but waiting is the hard part. Most people don't want to wait. This week put yourself in a position where you have to wait. Perhaps you'll file into the longest grocery line or drive the actual speed limit for a trip you'd usually speed through. Notice what happens as you slow down and as you wait. After a day of doing this, sit with yourself, by yourself, and recall your reactions to waiting. See if the Spirit may nudge you in a different direction.

Prayer

I want to live into your kingdom.
I want to produce something that's valuable.
I want to appreciate the value of others.
I want to love and not use people.
I want to steward what you've given.
I want those gifts to be for good and not evil.
Will you help me?
Will you keep me in the dark when I'm not ready for light?
Let me be a better person who represents you.
Thank you.

Blessing

There is a harvest in me.
I'll be faithful to nurture the gifts of God.
I'll be faithful to serve with those gifts.

Cultivating the Ability to Hear

With many such parables he spoke the word to them, as they were able to hear it. (Mark 4:33, ESV)

Mark, like the other gospels, is filled with parables, which was one of the forms Jesus used to teach. Though your reaction probably isn't the same, the original listeners experienced these stories, riddles, and metaphorical ways of speaking as you'd experience a joke that actually makes you laugh. Like Jesus' original audience and his teachings, you'd get it. You might smile; you might nod. You would understand what he was talking about and you'd get him. When I was growing up, people would ask, "You get my drift?" It was a way of checking in and confirming that you were heard. To answer yes was to say that you got it. Jesus' audience would hear his parables and get his drift.

For Jesus' listeners, and for you, getting it wasn't the issue. The issue was being able to hear it, and hearing it meant accepting it. Whether it was something about a sower, a lamp and a light, or a seed, the plainness of Jesus' words were startling—startling because they were so clear. There was little ambiguity. His teachings were undeniable. Trouble came with making the choice to *really* hear.

Isn't that the whole problem and opportunity of the spiritual life? Taking in what's clear, accepting what you already understand, integrating what you perceive, and obeying what you know deep within to be true. I would suggest that acceptance is simple, even though simple may not be easy. Once you know what Jesus is talking about, a choice is still a choice. You still have to say yes to something and no to something. You still have to follow him or go down a different path.

Instead of accepting the message of Jesus, some of his listeners blocked his message. Like many leaders who we adore after they depart, Jesus was not uniformly loved. It's hard to believe, but the man was hated by some. He certainly wasn't accepted by all. He isn't accepted by all now. Even you struggle with Jesus, right? You're reading a book about following him and you know well what it's like to *not* hear him, *not* listen to him, and *not* accept him. You know what it means to turn away from his parables. You and I can, at times, end those divine/simple stories before they're finished. You close off to the simple metaphors that open you to God. But they are there, waiting to be heard by your whole being. They are unrelenting.

Jesus continues to speak the word to you. I wonder if you can listen for a while. Jesus continues to have something to say to you, about you, and for you. "But I obey him," you may say. "I'm living my life for him." The beauty and wonder of Jesus is that he gives his life and speaks his words for those who don't do the same in return. What does it mean in your life, listening to and cultivating the ability to hear Jesus?

I think the answer is as simple as the deceptively simple teachings of Jesus. I think you cultivate the ability to hear by turning to Jesus. The ability to hear Jesus grows as you say regularly: "Jesus, I'm going to wait for you to speak." And then you do just that. You quiet yourself. You close your mouth. You wait.

You can't control if Jesus speaks. Of course, you can barely sit in quiet without the world of thoughts rushing upon you, vying for your attention. I know the feeling. But you can turn. I can turn. You can sit. You can commit to a time where you won't surf the web or where you won't watch your recorded shows or talk on the phone—to half the people on your contact list. You can control where and if you sit and listen. In this case, hearing comes after listening. Accepting the message comes as you hear that message, and you won't hear it without giving Jesus your attention.

Guiding Questions

1. What do you believe about how Jesus speaks to people?
2. Have you ever felt like God sent a person from heaven just to talk to you?
3. In your life, how have you surrendered to and rebelled against Jesus' words?

One Next Step

Think about where you spend your time and energy. Write those things down. Make a list of the things (or people) you give your love, energy, and attention. It may help to do this with a calendar so you can actually see where your time has gone. Notice those things. Consider what about each one grabs you, holds your attention, and keeps your interest.

Prayer

Speak to me.
Illuminate my world.
Draw new lines.
Expose hidden things.
Make truths plain.
Expand my vision.
Teach me.
Enliven me.
Draw me closer.
Let me hear.
Amen.

Blessing

I am capable of obeying Jesus.

The Spirit has given me all I need to follow Jesus.

I will.

Respect Your Fears

On that day, when evening had come, he said to them, "Let us go across to the other side." And leaving the crowd, they took him with them in the boat, just as he was. And other boats were with him. And a great windstorm arose, and the waves were breaking into the boat, so that the boat was already filling. But he was in the stern, asleep on the cushion. And they woke him and said to him, "Teacher, do you not care that we are perishing?" And he awoke and rebuked the wind and said to the sea, "Peace! Be still!" And the wind ceased, and there was a great calm. He said to them, "Why are you so afraid? Have you still no faith?" And they were filled with great fear and said to one another, "Who then is this that even wind and sea obey him?" (Mark 4:35-41, ESV)

What a silly question. That's my first and second reaction to a sleepy Jesus. Almost every time I read this passage, I immediately discount his crazy curiosity. I make excuses for Jesus. Perhaps he's sleep-deprived. After all, he's busy. He works miracles. He heals and preaches. He pulls together the strangest people and puts them in service. I want to believe that Jesus was tired when he woke and asked, "Why are you so afraid?" He couldn't have another reason to ask such a silly thing, could he?

Didn't he see the boat being broken by winds? Didn't he notice all the other boats, all those people yelling? Didn't he feel the wetness on his clothes? Of all the things he could say, Jesus asked a question that's so obvious it's unsettling: Why are you so afraid? And still, the question is rich.

It's rich, first, because his approach is to question them. Most people I know, including me, will walk into a crisis and start going about the work of resolving the crisis. I'm reminded of the trauma pages I've responded to in the hospital where I work. When there is a medical crisis, an entire group of people comes from all over the hospital to address the need. In our hospital when a trauma happens, a page is sent through the system to a rapid response team. Chaplains are part of the team so our on-call chaplain gets the page and responds within 5-10 minutes to the situation wherever it is on campus. The same team responds to cardiac arrests and visitors who fall unconscious.

Because our campus includes several buildings over several city blocks, it can take time to arrive at a trauma. It may take effort to leave a conversation as a spiritual caregiver, for instance. A doctor may need to leave a patient's room immediately. A nurse may need to grab a cart or a backpack and leave some things abruptly in the hands of a colleague. Some trauma calls turn out to be seizures, and seizures are different from cardiac events. Still, being a part of a rapid response assumes a readiness to encounter the worst. It assumes that we'll leave wherever we have been and that, after arriving, we're prepared to stick around and labor through what's next. You know and don't know what you'll see.

Jesus woke in a storm. He and his disciples were in their own traumatic situation. Alarmed, they called for him, paged him, and sought help. They thought they were dying. The writer described it as fear of perishing. They thought they were about to die. Jesus had to leave his rest to help them. He asks his disciples—in the middle of a crisis—a question. "What are you so afraid of?" In other words, what's at the bottom of your fear? By his own presence, Jesus was launching them into a physical reality that put their fears in the presence of a Lord who can sleep through a storm. There must be something sturdy present if Jesus could sleep. There must be some strength in him that enables those followers to answer that silly, rich question. I imagine you can think of things that God couldn't possibly sleep through, and I'm sure what you imagine it worth Jesus getting up to see. He is present. He is willing to be with you. He is willing to address what you fear.

Guiding Questions

1. How have you heard death described in your faith tradition?
2. What is fear?
3. What are the worst and best things about fear when you think of you and Jesus?

One Next Step

Make a list. Do it before you decide against it. Search your heart for what matters to you, the bad possibilities, the horrible options, the real fears. All those things that wake you up in the morning or keep you from falling asleep at night. They are the things that, when you're honest, are your answers to Jesus' question. Perhaps family members or work situations or past decisions are on your list. Get in touch with that list. Know what's on it. Now, imagine what Jesus might do with that list. When he woke up to it, what might he say?

Prayer

I hardly think about my fears.
I usually only feel them.
I rarely acknowledge them, respect them, and notice them.
Can I tap into what really moves me to worry?
Sit me down and counsel me about them.
Tell me where the fears come from.
Tell me what you think of them.
Talk to me about how I'll make it through the fright.
Bring me as much peace as you can.
Amen.

Blessing

I will live a life of surrender.
I will put my fears at the feet of Jesus.
I will live a life of courage.
I will face and conquer my fears with him.

One Image of Freedom

They came to the other side of the sea, to the country of the Gerasenes. And when Jesus had stepped out of the boat, immediately there met him out of the tombs a man with an unclean spirit. He lived among the tombs. And no one could bind him anymore, not even with a chain, for he had often been bound with shackles and chains, but he wrenched the chains apart, and he broke the shackles to pieces. No one had the strength to subdue him. Night and day among the tombs and on the mountains he was always crying out and bruising himself with stones. And when he saw Jesus from afar, he ran and fell down before him. (Mark 5:1-6, ESV)

Bound and unbound, chained and unchained, this man seemed destined to meet the healer. I read this passage and wonder if it was Jesus coming to the man or the man coming to Jesus. Mark has him falling before Jesus out of desperation. Whether Jesus knew he had to travel by the other side of the sea or whether this man, whose name we don't know, sensed his recovery close—there was a remarkable meeting between these two. One possessed the virtue to bless. The other had a pronounced need. However, even as I write this, I wonder if both men possessed both virtue and need.

For the unnamed man, no one's intervention worked. He was sick, ill in a dreadful and isolating way. At the time of his visit with Jesus, loneliness had cloaked him like a garment as he lived in the tombs. Quiet became his surrounding, undoubtedly opposing his interior noise. I imagine that he had not been spoken to anyone in a long time, though the text doesn't state that. I don't imagine him getting many visitors at the cemetery. Rather, I think of him as both internally ravaged and somehow hopeful. This could be my imagination alone, but I think of the man as lonely and accompanied. I think of him as finding solace in the place that he could, namely, the cemetery. He was not destitute, even if he was marginalized and too much to handle for soberly minded people. He was not without resources. After all, he did have a cemetery. And, he had himself.

    Healing, when it comes, is miraculous. It is incredible *and* clear. This person was isolated and bewildered and the Lord helped him. This healing paints a picture of God's normal living conditions. Different from the cemetery where the man had lived, Jesus delivered unto him how it is to live within the kingdom of God. Life in God's neighborhood connects you, frees you, and unburdens you. This image—the image of a free person connecting with friends—is a powerful picture of whole life in Christ. Does it appeal to you?

    But this is not the only image of freedom in the passage. To be pointed, Jesus, too, experienced freedom. He went to this man, received this man's desperation, and in doing so, was given a gift that no one else could take from him. This man's plea was in the ears of Jesus. What intimacy! To have this man's hopes falling before him,

Jesus was given an opportunity. This man blessed Jesus. I love Jesus. I respect Jesus. I know that Jesus is the One who heals. But this man, this unnamed man, was also a healer because he freed parts of Jesus in his worship, adoration, and surrender.

In this man's approach to Jesus *and* in Jesus' approach to him, these two met in a healing relationship. Both brought virtue. Both brought history. Both offered to the other what no one else could. That means that they were unique and that their uniqueness mattered.

Healing like this is uncomplicated, though it will cost you to have it. It will cost you your posture. You'll have to bend and maybe fall. You'll have to bless even as you seek your blessing because being a free giver always immediately comes with being a free receiver. In your life, you will have to look at living as your opportunity to offer Jesus something and not only your opportunity to receive. You have something for Jesus—in your cemetery, in your circumstance, in your isolation, in your location. Being like this man may get you healed *by* Jesus and it may also make you a gift-giver *to* Jesus.

Guiding Questions

1. What do you think of this view of Jesus receiving in this passage?
2. How have you been freed or healed in your life?
3. What does it mean to bless another person?

One Next Step

In step with Jesus, be intentional to offer someone a blessing. Make it as nuanced as you want it but keep in mind that blessings are usually simple, straight-forward words. Think of who you can bless and how you can bless the person. Don't give yourself reasons to back out. Choose one person, one comment. And walk in the footsteps of Jesus.

Prayer

You heal my afflictions.
You free me of bondage.
You join me in loneliness.
You arrive in my far-off places.
You bless me and delight in me.
You accept my worship.
You receive adoration from me.
You hear my words of blessing.
You love me and experience me as I am.
Thank you.
Amen.

Blessing

I am free for myself.
I am free for others.
I am free for God.

Becoming Generous

The herdsmen fled and told it in the city and in the country. And people came to see what it was that had happened. And they came to Jesus and saw the demon-possessed man, the one who had had the legion, sitting there, clothed and in his right mind, and they were afraid. And those who had seen it described to them what had happened to the demon-possessed man and to the pigs. And they began to beg Jesus to depart from their region. As he was getting into the boat, the man who had been possessed with demons begged him that he might be with him. And he did not permit him but said to him, "Go home to your friends and tell them how much the Lord has done for you, and how he has had mercy on you." And he went away and began to proclaim in the Decapolis how much Jesus had done for him, and everyone marveled. (Mark 5:14-20, ESV)

    I was 18 years old when I told my pastor that I didn't want to preach, and I did it publicly by walking on the stage and trying to reject the paper that was my license to do that very thing. I stood on that stage the Sunday after my high school graduation, during the largest worship service at our church. I remember shaking my head. I think I waved my hand as he spoke when he was introducing the idea to the congregation. I was a boy-preacher; but I was never really sold on the idea.

Something in me was incapable of seeing what that community saw.

Preaching requires the ability to see and when that sight isn't present, you do what I did. *You run*. Sharing faith can be intimidating. After all, aren't there things to learn, words to memorize, scriptures to quote? As importantly, isn't sharing the same as preaching? There are people who do that and people who don't, right? I was one of those people trying not to preach, trying to be clear about who I wanted to be and how that rubbed against what other people saw in me. I didn't want to preach and I was pretty close to not wanting to share either! I wasn't generous.

Preachers preach, but the example of this passage is so much more basic than segmenting a group who does something that others don't. Telling people about Jesus is more common than spectacular. Here's a clue that isn't a clue: faith sharing is always giving away what God has given you in your life. It's not special and it is special. It's not special in the sense of exclusivity. "Only a certain number of people do this." And it is special in that sharing faith is unique to your experience with Jesus, in your life. Your life belongs to you, not to me.

Don't get side-tracked by the exciting work of God in the man living in the cemetery. We can't all live near graves. But this story shows that his experience with God was what he pulled from in order to "go" and to "tell." His time among the graves set him up for however he would discuss what happened to him. The context of his life served as the introduction to his meeting with Jesus, and that encounter would frame the testimony he shared about his transformation.

After the ministry, the man is known by who he was, who he had been, and what he had struggled with. The gospel is subject to this sad use of the unnamed man. Even within our sacred scriptures, this man is not far from his yesterday. In one sense, it's unfortunate that his story stayed with him. He would always be associated with then. On the other hand, it was his story that allowed him to effectively proclaim Jesus. Just by showing up, fully clothed and not naked, contemplative and not impulsive, settled and not thrashing about; just by entering a room, he was a testimony to God's mercy.

If there are things noticed about you when you show up, perhaps, old and embarrassing details, there is a claim present, evidence of mercy. Go home to be a witness. Return to your old stomping grounds and give away what God has done to you, in you, and for you. Do what I couldn't when I was a preacher: accept your license.

Guiding Questions

1. How would this unnamed man look in your neighborhood today?
2. What are the ways Jesus expressed generosity in this passage?
3. Where can you be generous this week with your story about God?

One Next Step

This step is in step with the reflections above. Following Jesus is dialogical. It involves you telling others about the work of Jesus in you. It is not preachy, but it does follow naturally when Jesus is at work. After each day this week, think through where you've been open about your faith. That openness is implicit and also explicit, behavioral and verbal. At the end of each day, notice where you've spoken about your spiritual life and where you haven't. There are other steps and the first is noticing.

Prayer

Generous describes you. Make me open-handed with what I have. Mercy marks you. Help me to be compassionate in every way. You wait for me to ready for my change. Grant me the patience to wait with others. My change has taken time, and is taking time. Slow me down to appreciate in what you're doing in others. Turn me into a generous person. Make the world around me better because of me. Amen.

Blessing

I am a recipient of grace and a giver of grace.
I have received, and I will give.
Sometimes just by showing up.

When Following Looks Like Leading

And when Jesus had crossed again in the boat to the other side, a great crowd gathered about him, and he was beside the sea. Then came one of the rulers of the synagogue, Jairus by name, and seeing him, he fell at his feet and implored him earnestly saying, "My little daughter is at the point of death. Come and lay your hands on her, so that she may be made well and live. And he went with him. (Mark 5:21-24, ESV)

I grew as a boy who *everybody* said would preach. And everybody was right. Eventually. But I didn't start ministry by preaching. I began by following the leaders. I learned as a child that preachers didn't start by preaching. I learned that leaders are made from followers. Two things stand out in that lesson. First, everybody follows. Leaders get used to leading in the school of following, so that anyone who becomes a leader first follows. Second, is something I hinted at and it is that leaders are made. Leaders don't come ready-made. They're developed.

This passage offers this dual-sided glimpse into discipleship. Jairus turns into the leader. Jesus turns into the follower. Both men would likely have assumed the opposite role for the other. Jesus, the teacher and healer, was usually asked for the application of his power. People asked him to heal because he was the one who healed. That's what he did. Jesus was the rabbi so people followed him. Eventually that happened in Jairus' experience. He, too, would follow. Still, Jesus also followed Jairus. The leader of leaders, Jesus turned to walk after a man in trouble. He was a follower.

Jairus, a man of authority, approached Jesus expecting to ask for something. In his asking, he had to exercise faith and leadership by taking Jesus home. In those acts, he was someone different than who generally was. Of course, he was a religious leader. He knew how to lead. But, leading Jesus? Imagine this man as he approached the place where Jesus was. Dealing with all his questions and fears, there was likely a monologue in his head. He might have second-guessed himself. He may have questioned his introduction. He likely went back and forth about how much to say when he finally arrived to meet the Healer.

Both men, Jesus and Jairus, had to release their older, well-used expectations. Jairus had to lead Jesus. Jesus, before healing the girl, had to follow Jairus. Imagine what part of the healing process would not have happened if one or both of them decided to stick with their old scripts. If Jesus said, "I'll heal the girl from here," how many people would have missed the displayed goodness of God? If Jairus had not bravely led the Healer, what wouldn't he have walked away with about his own strengths in a crisis? Both these men saw new things because they did something different. They both walked deeper into life with God because they accepted a new role. Both were willing to see following in a new way.

These movements may seem like stretches but they hold in relief what following looks like. Following

Jesus means turning away from old expectations. It looks like taking risks. Following looks like becoming a leader when you expect to be the follower. It looks like humbly taking a different role than the one you usually take.

Jesus exhibits a kind of mutuality that I admire. He's not only willing to go with Jairus but he actually *follows* him. Jairus, worth admiring too, steps up with a boldness to lead Jesus for a while. That courageous leadership is a reflection of what Jesus loved about people who followed. They were willing to do what was needed to get Jesus to come.

This image of Jesus may not feel immediately approachable to you. It may be hard to imagine Jesus following you, especially in a book about *following him*. My point is that Jesus is qualified to lead you because he is humble enough to follow you. He'll go into your life wherever you need him. Notice those places, those soul-places where you need healing or help. Invite the Healer to accompany you home. Perhaps, by extending that invitation, you will learn more about who you really are. Maybe in "leading Jesus for a while," you'll come to see yourself differently.

Guiding Questions

1. If you could take Jesus anywhere, where would you go?
2. What unsettles you about this passage and reflection?
3. How is your heart stirred by Jairus' courage?

One Next Step

Take Jesus on a tour of your neighborhood. This may mean taking a stroll or a drive. It may mean visiting the places you frequent when you errand. Do any of these types of things in the company of Jesus or with increasing awareness of his company. Ask Jesus to walk with you, see with you, and follow you as you go about a day. Slow down in order to point to things you'd like him to attend to, and see if you can tell Jesus a story about why what you're showing him matters.

Prayer

Open my eyes so I can see what following means. Make me available to follow in head, heart, and hands. I'm available. I'm willing. I'm already facing you. I'll risk what I need to risk. I'll bend where I must bend. I want to follow you no matter it takes. Amen.

Blessing

Risk what you will.
Gain how you will.
Go where you will.
All in the power of the Spirit.

Getting Everything You Need

And there was a woman in the crowd who had had a hemorrhage for twelve years. She had suffered a great deal from many doctors through the years and had spent everything she had to pay them, but she had gotten no better. In fact, she was worse. She had heard about Jesus, so she came up behind him through the crowd and touched the fringe of his robe. For she thought to herself, "If I can just touch his clothing, I will be healed." Immediately the bleeding stopped, and she could feel that she had been healed! Jesus realized at once that healing power had gone out from him, so he turned around in the crowd and asked, "Who touched my clothes?" His disciples said to him, "All this crowd is pressing around you. How can you ask, 'Who touched me?'" But he kept on looking around to see who had done it. Then the frightened woman, trembling at the realization of what had happened to her, came and fell at his feel and told him what she had done. And he said to her, "Daughter, your faith has made you well. Go in peace. You have been healed." (Mark 5:25-34, ESV)

God does not always grant your request but your request is always worth offering. The inherent danger to following Jesus is not knowing what God will give you when you make a request. That's reason enough to turn your desires into prayers. You never know. You might be surprised! Of course, if you already think you know what

God will do, test your theory. But be careful not to be too self-assured. Sometimes not knowing what you're talking about is a good thing.

In the previous meditation, you saw Jairus take a risk. In this passage, you read the sister doing the same thing. She's doing the unexpected. She's up to no good from one point of view. Unclean, ritually, it was said that she had no business going out in public. Yet, this is exactly what she does. She goes against the grain, against convention, and probably against her own conscience. She goes against these things in order to pursue healing.

She had no money she had lost that. Really, she spent it. She spent her money in the same direction, toward her healing. Her risk tolerance was high. Of course, by the time she came onto this noisy scene and into this bustling crowd, she only had her inner poise left. Unsure whether Jesus would heal her, she risked all that remained—the bits of pride in her inner spirit—to achieve her miracle. The shining ray of her humanity met with God's kingdom glory on display. Kingdom glory equaled her wholeness. It was glorious because it meant her being whole, reconnected to what she lost, nourished after having spent what mattered.

I don't think this passage could have ended without this woman getting what she needed. Unlike many in the Bible, she put it all on the line to get healed. She gave it all in order to be blessed. She spent and gave and traveled and worked. What I love about this story is that, in this case, all her efforts paid off.

I know that everyone's story doesn't end this way. Everybody doesn't get healed. Not everybody walks away with what they've prayed and fasted and waited for. But this woman does. That's the part I love. If God could work in her life, the story has legs.

The story can mean something for you. The story might suggest that you don't have to stay broken. You can be healed. At least, you can pursue it. You may not have it at the moment. Your spirit may be dazed and you may be too rattled to move in the direction of healing. Give yourself what you need, even if that looks like silence, time away, or sitting still. Know that if you want to get healed, if you want to walk the path this sister walked, it is available.

You don't know how God will answer. And that's a good thing. You could still join the company of this sister. You could be among those who are blessed with exactly what you've spent everything to get. Wouldn't you keep going just to see? Wouldn't you join the little girl Jesus raised and the woman from this passage?

Guiding Questions

1. What's the most trouble you've gotten into to pursue something you wanted?
2. How has social convention privileged you and how has it constrained you?
3. Does your gender play a part in your role in the world?

One Next Step

      Tell yourself a story about how you got to where you are. Choose one part of your story and think it through. Perhaps you'll write it down, put it to music, or develop a poem. Include the people who entrusted their hopes with you, the people who inspired and motivated you. Include the people who you trusted and who betrayed you. There are people who "took your money" but didn't better you. And there are people who were God's agents in your story. Think of them. Tell yourself a part of the story about how you've been healed.

Prayer

Where did I learn that I had to stop short of what I wanted?

Who taught me that I couldn't have my wholeness?

Where did my conception of a stingy God come from?

Did I learn early on that I mattered to you and to the world?

Did I get convinced that I was poor, insufficient, and lacking?
What did I grow up with that influenced me to think this couldn't be mine?

How could I grow to my age and not know I was necessary?

Will you begin to walk me through the answers to these questions?

Amen.

Blessing

I'm going for it.
I'm bringing others along.
I'm partnering with people so that we're all blessed.

Enriching the Meeting

While he was still speaking to her, messengers arrived from Jairus's home with the message, "Your daughter is dead. There's no use troubling the Teacher now." But Jesus ignored their comments and said to Jairus, "Don't be afraid. Just trust me." Then Jesus stopped the crowd and wouldn't let anyone go with him except Peter and James and John. When they came to the home of the synagogue leader, Jesus saw the commotion and the weeping and wailing. He went inside and spoke to the people. "Why all this weeping and commotion?" he asked. "The child isn't dead; she is only asleep." The crowd laughed at him, but he told them all to go outside. Then he took the girl's father and mother and his three disciples into the room where the girl was lying. Holding her hand, he said to her, "Get up, little girl!" And the girl, who was twelve years old, immediately stood up and walked around! Her parents were absolutely overwhelmed. Jesus commanded them not to tell anyone what had happened, and he told them to give her something to eat. (Mark 5:35-43, ESV)

I don't think it's always helpful to think about the gospels in terms of mimicking Jesus. Jesus did things we cannot do. I think of Jesus as God incarnate, as God in the flesh, and because of that I see his ability as different from mine or yours. His abilities go beyond mine. He's able to accomplish more than you. That's the way I see him. He's not you. He's not me.

On the other hand, there is a way that Jesus offers a path to walk, a way of being. He is, after all, in the flesh. He's a person, too. One thing that means is that as he lives he generates life. His life leads to life. Following him ends with life. In other words, if you follow Jesus, you'll live, you'll experience life, and you'll get acquainted with strength. The same is true when you live the way Jesus lived. Living the Jesus way and walking the path that Jesus carved means replicating life.

This passage provides a display for what life looks like. You see in this story that life looks like continued living, ripples of living. Jairus had pled with Jesus to return to his sick daughter, and he walked with Jesus in the direction of where the child lay dying. Jairus received word of her death, and it's easy to imagine his broken spirit. This father had done his best to get Jesus to attend to his daughter and he failed. I imagine Jairus feeling sharp grief, deep judgment, and broadening hopelessness. And still life was alive, still moving.

In an almost incredible way, Jesus encouraged Jairus to trust him. That's his response, and I'm sure he said so in a sensitive, delicate way. How else can it go over so well? It couldn't have come as a simple answer, as a dry cliché. In his words and in his tone, whatever his tone, Jesus was modeling for Jairus what it meant to be trustworthy. Jesus was able to model for this grief-stricken father what he needed.

You and I need this from time to time as well: a person who is stable. Jesus kept walking with Jairus, assured in himself that he could meet the girl's need. Now, back to the mimicking that I mentioned because this is one of those opportunities you can draw from Jesus, mimic him, and live like him. You have gifts and abilities to heal others and to bless people when they most need God. Having been gifted by God, you can be stable for the distraught. You can walk with people in the midst of grief. You can enrich their lives at their most vulnerable moments. In the interaction between you and them, you can enrich the meeting.

Imagine being in that house with Jairus and his wife. Perhaps see yourself being in the role of one of those Jesus invited to stay. There was the girl, the mother and father, and there were the three disciples. Jesus raised the girl. Wonder, no doubt spilled into the room as life returned to her eyes and as clarity arrived in her parents. They saw that God blessed her with healing and raised her from death. If you were present in your imagination, wouldn't that motivate your next step? I think that vision would capture you and leave you with goods to give to others.

Guiding Questions

1. Consider for a moment what Jesus actually did in that room.
2. How might you enrich someone's life by following in the way of Jesus?

3. What difference does Jesus make in your life these days?

One Next Step

Tell everyone. Unlike Jesus' admonishment to those in Jairus' home, "tell no one"— you have an opportunity to resist keeping quiet. You have a chance to consider what Jesus has done and to share it. If you find sharing experiences easy, you'll love this step. If you find it hard, sharing may be a challenge. Either way, think of this next step as a chance to expose people to a thing God did, to a thing God said, or to a gift God gave you. Perhaps there's less pressure when you're telling everyone or anyone about a gift. Pick one person and start with one person.

Prayer

When I want to be quiet about what you've done, embolden me. When I'm lost in my head and unsure of you, remind me. When I'm cold to the needs of others, warm me. When I feel impatient with myself, center me. When I find it taxing to serve others, inspire me. When I can't seem to locate you, locate me. When I see others sharing stories about you, encourage me. Amen.

Blessing

There is nothing preventing me from blessing others.

I'm going for it.

I'm following Jesus.

Leaving Home

He went away from there and came to his hometown, and his disciples followed him. And on the Sabbath he began to teach in the synagogue, and many who heard him were astonished, saying, "Where did this man get these things? What is the wisdom given to him? How are such mighty works done by his hands? Is not this the carpenter, the son of Mary and brother of James and Joses and Judas and Simon? And are not his sisters here with us?" And they took offense at him. And Jesus said to them, "A prophet is not without honor, except in his hometown and among his relatives and in his own household." And he could do no mighty work there, except that he laid his hands on a few sick people and healed them. And he marveled because of their unbelief. And he went about among the villages teaching. (Mark 6:1-6, ESV)

Mark describes several scenes where Jesus exerts authority over sickness, demons, weather, and silly people. Because of Mark's descriptions, Jesus looks pretty good at the start of this chapter. But his pride, if Jesus has any, pushes against a reality check: his hometown. Jesus came from ministry and returned home.

Like everyone Jesus had a hometown. Capernaum was its name, and it's the only place that writers of scripture call home base for Jesus. After Capernaum, Jesus wouldn't have another. And this passage shows Jesus returning, finding no honor, and leaving home. In his experience rests something everyone knows to varying degrees. A person can always return home and at the same time, there is something essentially upsetting about staying there.

      When Jesus returned to Capernaum, some people did not accept him. Regardless of the miracles and the ways his name spread. Regardless of the real good he accomplished. To some, Jesus was unremarkable, even unacceptable. Notice what Jesus did when he was rejected by his relatives, by his extended family. He tried. He knew the town and the people. He tried to minister. I imagine that Jesus saw the responses coming. After all, he knew the town. He knew his kin. Mark's passage says that Jesus said a few things, left, and did what he could where he could.

      Still, he tried. He was probably moved by his hometown, and the text says he marveled. To my reading, he was shaken and what I think of as being upset in an essential way. If you read the whole book of Mark, you'll find that Jesus' life moved toward his death and resurrection. His gait was steady. Being rejected didn't stop him, even if he made him wonder. If anything, leaving Capernaum (i.e., leaving home) meant that Jesus could advance toward that known point and that other place called Golgotha. Golgotha would not be a new home. It was a place like Samaria or Sidon where Jesus had to visit. It was like the region of the Gadarenes where he would minister. He would not have visited those places, served those people, and provided you with a view into the kingdom of God had he not left Capernaum.

Think of what leaving home means for you. It will necessarily involve some upset. Leaving always does. You may leave under a cloud of mystery. You may run away. You may be called away, convinced by some noble need in the world. Perhaps it isn't what calls you from home but the act of leaving that's worth holding to as you consider departing. It will plant you into a community of persons who leave just like you. Everyone departs; everyone goes. At some point, for some reason, everyone leaves home. When you grow, you will leave home. As you age, leaving looks more and more natural. You aren't alone in going. There are others who have done what you will need to do. There are others who have left notes and secrets to the journeys ahead.

When Jesus left Capernaum, he had a sense of what he was heading toward. I'm not sure he saw the entire picture. For instance, I'm not sure he saw what returning to his ultimate home at his Father's side would look like. He had never died. He had never experienced resurrection. He had no previous experience with re-entering glory with a body much less one that had been raised. But he did take a step to leave the town he knew. Walk with him when you next have the choice to stay or go. You'll be accompanied in that journey. You'll be by the side of Jesus.

Guiding Questions

1. What has Jesus taught you recently?
2. Considering people, places, and things, where have you left in your life?
3. How might the examples of others bring you courage for your upcoming departures?

One Next Step

     If following Jesus is about joining a community of people who leave, take courage in that community. Investigate the stories of others who have left to follow Jesus. Consider the decisions before you, the places or relationships that feel like (or are) home to you. If the Spirit has been stirring upsetting movements in you, perhaps you might read or listen to the stories of others who have decided to follow God in their going. Look around. Who has left and what can they teach you?

Prayer

Give me the strength to choose.
Give me the vision to see.
Give me the boldness to go.
Give me the space to grieve.
Give me the openness to accept.
Give me the patience to adjust.
Give me the gift your company.
When it's time, enable me to leave.
Amen.

Blessing

Wherever I go in my life, I have a home.
I have acceptance, compassion, enjoyment, and disciplined love in my future.

Dealing with John's Death

King Herod heard of it, for Jesus' name had become known. Some said, "John the Baptist has been raised from the dead. That is why these miraculous powers are at work in him." But others said, "He is Elijah." And others said, "He is a prophet, like one of the prophets of old." But when Herod heard of it, he said, "John, whom I beheaded, has been raised." For it was Herod who had sent and seized John and bound him in prison for the sake of Herodias, his brother Philip's wife, because he had married her. For John had been saying to Herod, "It is not lawful for you to have your brother's wife." And Herodias had a grudge against him and wanted to put him to death. But she could not, for Herod feared John, knowing that he was a righteous and holy man, and he kept him safe. When he heard him, he was greatly perplexed, and yet he heard him gladly...And the king was exceedingly sorry, but because of his oaths and his guests he did not want to break his word to her. And immediately the king sent an executioner with orders to bring John's head. He went and beheaded him in the prison and brought his head on a platter and gave it to the girl, and the girl gave it to her mother. When his disciples heard of it, they came and took his body and laid it in a tomb. (Mark 6:14-29, ESV)

This is a long passage to read with many elements to appreciate. After reading mine, you might consider your own thoughts since there's so much in the story. I'll give you one of mine. It's about John's murder.

John did not, simply, die. He was put to death. That's the frame for this story: Herod putting John to death. The forerunner's death was frightening, terrible, and sad. And it didn't have to happen. Such events aren't attractive but they are common. His murder makes his death memorable in a deep way.

That said, John's death was no less significant than Jesus' death, even though we preach for weeks and weeks about one death and generally pass over the other. This story stands up as a witness to observe the unobservable, to attend to what can be missed. As a Christian, I wonder if a person can truly appreciate what happens to Jesus without appreciating what happened to John. He was murdered, killed not for the salvific purposes applied to Jesus' death but for something less. That is its own burdensome grief. John died for less. He died for entertainment and lack of strength.

Moreover, the king knew John to be a righteous man, a man worth protecting, a man worth hearing. But the king was not persuaded by his own mind. Herod had protected John. In doing so, he behaved outside of his own mind. By his own view, the forerunner was a man to be regarded. Herod listened to what he had to say, a gesture showing how much Herod must have respected John's message. After all, John was telling Herod, in part, about his sins.

I want to be careful not to say that a person should never change his mind. Herod could have changed his mind. I believe that happens all the time. As I come to this text and see Herod act against his mind, I'm sensitive to why he changed *his course* toward John. He did not change his perspective about John. He never changed his mind about John. Perplexed when he heard the preacher, he continued to listen. By the party, when he promised to give his brother's wife whatever she wanted, he was sorry. He knew then that he'd have to act against what he knew or risk embarrassment. Doing so, acting against his best thought—which was to respect John and hear him—Herod enacted a tragic death. Not only did John die, but the reasons underpinning John's death also exhibited Herod losing the thread of his own conscience.

    Herod set aside his thinking concerning John and gave a little girl and a sinister woman the power that was *his* to exercise. The added weight of John's execution was in Herod killing him against his own conscience. A good man died because of a promise made in a drunken state. All of this is worth remembering when dealing with John's death. We have to deal with the circumstances leading to that death. Indeed, sitting with John's death, as it was, will help you sit in the dismal times that you might miss. You might carry this reflection with you as you count the deaths that pass your television, your screen, or your eyes. You may pray differently and ask God to help you deal with those deaths in a new way.

Guiding Questions

1. How often does death happen around you, in your city, or in your community?
2. What do you believe is God's response to one person's death at the hands of another?
3. Contrast the ways you've heard John's death and Jesus' death discussed?

One Next Step

Bow your head for thirty seconds when you hear of the death of someone. Whether or not you know them, consider them and consider their loved ones. This is one way to acknowledge that those persons, whatever the circumstances of their lives and their deaths, matter. You may develop other specific acts to acknowledge the power of death for those persons, but choose this first act to embody, ritualize, and point to who those persons were. They were once here and now they're gone. Next, imagine the ways in which a loving Jesus responds. Then choose yours.

Prayer

Make sure I remember John. Make sure I recall why he died. His life and his death matter and they capture the reason for Jesus' life and death. May I never forget the people who die. May I bring peace to their memories. May I, by my living, refuse to let death remove their meaning. May I follow Jesus by these life-giving acts. Amen.

Blessing

I will offer life to everyone I meet.
I will refuse to see death the same.
I will bring life.

"I'm Here."

Immediately he made his disciples get into the boat and go before him to the other side, to Bethsaida, while he dismissed the crowd. And after he had taken leave of them, he went up on the mountain to pray. And when evening came, the boat was out on the sea, and he was alone on the land. And he saw that they were making headway painfully, for the wind was against them. And about the fourth watch of the night he came to them, walking on the sea. He meant to pass by them, but when they saw him walking on the sea they thought it was a ghost, and cried out, for they all saw him and were terrified. But immediately he spoke to them and said, "Take heart; it is I. Do not be afraid." And he got into the boat with them, and the wind ceased. And they were utterly astounded, for they did not understand about the loaves, but their hearts were hardened. (Mark 6:45-52, ESV)

The disciples didn't understand much of what Jesus said. His parables confused them. Some of his comebacks required explanation. Even though he worked words with simplicity and profundity, the disciples didn't always get him. I imagine that this was one of those times.

Mark describes the group as utterly astounded. It's interesting given how clear Jesus' teachings usually were. I can imagine the disciples thinking of what they'd heard earlier, seeing again how Jesus worked with loaves of bread. Wet with water slapping them because of great winds, Jesus said to them then what he had said before, words that were affirming and clear and misunderstood. Don't fear.

Don't be afraid. Calm yourself. Lighten up. Guard your heart. Stop worrying. Think about something else. Slow down. Breathe deeply. Synonyms, all of them, and they add up to "I'm here." The One they knew to be savior made himself known, spoke rest to the winds, and joined them in their boat. Jesus himself was in the words of encouragement. He's there, telling them not to worry. Don't be afraid because of the presence of Jesus.

I'm stumped by the fact that Jesus hoped to pass by his disciples. He had intended, presumably, to walk by them without stopping. Did he know this group? Was he familiar with them? Surely, he knew they were the jumpy kind. I wonder if Mark's portrayal, here, is accurate. Walking by, what could Jesus have thought he would accomplish? Didn't he know they needed him to stop by and not pass by?

Walking by. Passing by. I feel this phrase as a burden when I'm at my worst. Sometimes I feel like Jesus intends to pass by when I'm experiencing pain and bitter wind. Sometimes I feel like Jesus makes a second choice to stop when he had planned to go right by. Sometimes I feel like Jesus keeps going by and doesn't stop at all. I'll admit how grateful I am to have this story, if for no reason other than that Jesus, against his first mind, stops. As much as I question Mark's statement that Jesus planned to pass by,

I'm thankful that I have this example of him stopping because of their fear.

It says to me that you can be fearless because he is near. It's a reminder that your strength, however strong it seems, finds its bottom in him. You don't create your own fearlessness. You receive it. It's in the presence of Jesus who is with you as life flies by, as the winds of your days build in furor. While those things happen, Jesus is there. You may feel alone. You may feel left and abandoned. This story provides a relief and a message against those feelings. You are not alone. Jesus speaks and says, "Don't be afraid. I'm here."

You can study your fears, see where they start, and see where they're headed. Their power is limited in the company of Jesus. So, hear his voice this week saying to you, in words that sound understandable, "I'm here. Do not fear." Look at the crashing waves or the boisterous winds. Resist the urge to shrink in that weather trying to claim your soul. Breathe and blink until you see the shadowy figure of a God coming for you. That figure will respond to you, and you'll recognize the Presence.

Guiding Questions

1. How do you stay calm in a crisis?
2. What helps you feel less fearful?
3. What role does Jesus play in addressing your fears?

One Next Step

Study your fears as I suggested in the reflection above. Notice themes if you can. Track when and where you are especially able to sense the company of Jesus and when you aren't. Perhaps you'll see patterns. Consider sharing what you see as you study with someone you trust.

Prayer

One of my fears is that you won't be there,
That you aren't telling the truth about being with me,
And that I'll be alone when I need you most.

If I trace this fear, it starts with other moments of being left. This fear begins with having been told I'd be accompanied when I wasn't.

Deal with me and notice those moments with grace. Review those times as I review them. Tell me your experience of my previous pains. Tell me how to trust your presence. Show me what I need to see in order to believe you. Feed me through this. Nourish my whole self in this. Amen.

Blessing

I have all I need to trust God's presence.
I have the capacity to see.
I have the capacity to believe.
I have the capacity to trust.

Becoming Hard or Becoming Humble

Now when the Pharisees gathered to him, with some of the scribes who had come from Jerusalem, they saw that some of his disciples ate with hands that were defiled, that is, unwashed. (For the Pharisees and all the Jews do not eat unless they wash their hands, holding to the tradition of the elders, and when they come from the marketplace, they do not eat unless they wash. And there are many other traditions that they observe, such as the washing of cups and pots and copper vessels and dining couches.) And the Pharisees and the scribes asked him, "Why do your disciples not walk according to the tradition of the elders, but eat with defiled hands?" And he said to them, "Well did Isaiah prophesy of you hypocrites, as it is written, 'This people honors me with their lips, but their heart is far from me; in vain do they worship me, teaching as doctrines the commandments of men.' You leave the commandment of God and hold to the tradition of men." And he said to them, "You have a fine way of rejecting the commandment of God in order to establish your tradition! For Moses said, "Honor your father and your mother'; and Whoever reviles father or mother must surely die.' But you say, 'If a man tells his father or his mother, Whatever you would have gained from me is Corban' (that is, given to God)— then you no longer permit him to do anything for his father or mother, thus making void the word of God by your tradition that you have handed down. And many such things you do." (Mark 7:1-13, ESV)

The idea of following what Jesus says stands on the premise that what Jesus says is worth following, that there is weight, heft, and remarkable meaning in his words. His words are able to loosen you from your hardened places. Old wounds. Past failures. Feelings of soul-shame. Beliefs that you aren't adored by God. Jesus can lift your soul places you never thought would move. When your heart tells you in quiet and loud voices who you aren't and what you aren't, Jesus can convince you of things in your heart. In other words, Jesus can change how you interpret God and how you interpret you.

In a similar way, the Pharisees in this passage gave weight to their interpretations of the text. They weren't unlike you and me. We give weight to our views of scripture. You probably know people who hold too tightly to their interpretations of scripture, tightly enough to have you worry over their devotion to the God to which the text points. That said, even the presupposition that the way Jesus views a text is more important than a person's reading of a text is an interpretation. It's one of my presuppositions, right? It's something I come to the terms with before reading the text.

I think the issue is beyond that. I think Jesus pushes us to question ourselves, to question our proximity to our convictions, to question how hardened we've allowed ourselves to become. Sure, this text is specific. There's language about honoring God, about commandments, about parents. There are specifics worth wondering into, and then there is the bottom of it all, which seems to be whether we're even open to such specific matters. This is what I mean by becoming humble. Humility in this regard is being open to difference and, particularly, being open to seeing things differently. It's openness to dropping what you believe.

If Jesus tells you to think differently, are you open to doing that? Are you open to seeing something in your family differently? Can you give up your developed and considered opinion about your religious life? Such questions are fundamentally about whether Jesus has the right to change you. You might cling to your points of view. You might not be able to follow Jesus in *that* area. You might be considerably open in one respect and not another. Doesn't knowing that about yourself feel freeing? God certainly knows what you have yet to accept as true about yourself. God knows what you have yet to accept about Jesus. It's a part of God being God.

Below, in the guiding questions, are three questions I'd suggest you ponder when coming to your beliefs and your sacred texts. They emerge out of my reading of this passage in Mark. I commend them to you as you consider potentially changing how you see and what meaning you make of your sacred passages. Perhaps Jesus has something to say about you seeing.

Guiding Questions

1. Am I willing to accept whatever this says about me, even if it's unsettling?
2. What will enable me to distance myself from my older ways of seeing in order to see something else, however scary or new?
3. What would it look like for me to *do* what God says in this passage, regardless of my "beliefs"?

One Next Step

Invite a person who you believe loves Jesus the way you do and who you disagree with on some theological points to tea. Sit down and talk about how you both approach the scriptures. Be motivated to listen. Hear in that conversation how you both come to your sacred writings. Appreciate that person's approach, and appreciate your own approach. Both of you come at the scriptures from wonderful distances.

Prayer

I am unsatisfied with my mediocre approach to life.
I want to turn toward you completely. If that means giving some things, people, and beliefs up, I will. I may not like it; in fact, I won't like it. But I will do it in order to become. Make me who I am. Make me who you know me to be. Take the fragile beginnings in my soul and create the person I am. Amen.

Blessing

I am open to whatever God wants to do in me.
If that means I'll be different, I welcome being different.

Starting Within

And he called the people to him again and said to them, "Hear me, all of you, and understand: There is nothing outside a person that by going into him can defile him, but the things that come out of person are what defile him." And when he had entered the house and left the people, his disciples asked him about the parable. And he said to them, "Then, are you also without understanding? Do you not see that whatever goes into a person from outside cannot defile him, since it enters not his heart but his stomach, and is expelled?" (Thus he declared all foods clean.) And he said, "What comes out of a person is what defiles him. For from within, out of the heart of man, come evil thoughts, sexual immorality, theft, murder, adultery, coveting, wickedness, deceit, sensuality, envy, slander, pride, foolishness. All these evil things come from within, and they defile a person. (Mark 7:14-23, ESV)

  I don't like being told what to do. And, maybe it's because I grew up being told what to do. Most of the time, it was my mother telling me what to do. My father joined in, and my older sister and brother did, too. Our church also had its way of telling me what to do. Of course, the church told other children what to do. I wasn't alone in that. I noticed then that adults tend to tell children what to do. Specifically, growing up for me meant a fair bit of people focusing on my behavior. I've grown to appreciate this because I tell our sons what to do. I've gotten good at it!

Nonetheless, behaviors are externals. They are observable and noticeable, and behaviors are ways we gauge progress, learning, and growth. External behaviors matter. At the same time, the externals don't go deep enough to change you. They only go so far. Something else matters, something more important. I wonder if you can start right there, recognizing that all your religious acts and all my religious expressions are, at best, external attempts at something else that really matters. All your behaviors are about what Jesus turns his listeners and his followers to: the heart. Jesus turns people away from the obvious externals and toward the internal. The heart is what opens or closes to God.

The heart serves as God's guide to knowing who you are and to naming you. Your heart—your unseen interiority—is where your character shapes, develops, grows, and emerges. To speak of your heart is to speak of the you that's unseen. It's a metaphor for something that can't be captured in a word, but you get the idea. What matters is what eventually changes, corrupts, alters, and makes you, but it doesn't start on a platter atop a table. It doesn't begin with a behavior your loved ones can see or correct or challenge. You don't start with behavior. You start within. Evil thoughts, and the long list Jesus gives, start inside. Jesus lifts up interiority.

Read that last verse again. "All these evil things come from within, and they defile a person." These evil inside things are impossible to notice. The good, inside things are impossible to notice, too—until you *behave yourself*. Nobody sees these inside things in themselves. Like me, you need somebody to point these evils out, somebody who has lived with you or seen you behave. A roommate. A child. A spouse. A co-worker. A person on the street. You need people who the Spirit resides in and who God uses to show you *you*.

Those people are paying attention to you, seeing your "inside" on display. Next time someone points out something you'd "never do," take a breath before responding. Then, before you speak, whisper a one line prayer, something like, "God, is that really in me?" Even if you respond to the person before hearing God's answer, that's an opening. Expect God to get the point across, and try to open your ears to an answer. That's the whole point: to change you and your terrible heart—or to keep that already lovely heart on the path to becoming lovelier.

Guiding Questions

1. What are some of your good inside-things and what are some of your bad ones?
2. How do you cultivate your interiority?
3. When do you recall opening yourself to God recently?

One Next Step

Express gratitude to God for who you are and how he has made you. Thanking God for the good in you is an act of worship. It's fitting to repent of your evil insides. Confession of evil is necessary to follow Jesus, and it is also necessary to speak of the good insides that God's nurtured within you. In your own way, thank God for who you are. You are more than the bad or the negative or the sin. You are good. Spot that goodness and praise God for it. You'll be doing what God does! You'll be acting like God, being honest, being open, and being thankful.

Prayer

Search me and then help me to search myself. I don't want to take your place in searching my own heart. But I do want the ability to be honest about myself. I want to be humble enough to see what's real about me. Grant me the power to see who I am. Grant me the power to state who I am. Grant me the power to praise you for making me good. Grant me the strength to notice my evils *and* my goods. Grant me the faith that you're already, always working with both. Help me accept you. Help me accept me. Amen.

Blessing

I am flawed and I am worthy.
I will be open to God's experience of me in both.

Love on Display

Then he returned from the region of Tyre and went through Sidon to the Sea of Galilee, in the region of the Decapolis. And they brought to him a man who was deaf and had a speech impediment, and they begged him to lay his hand on him. And taking him aside from the crowd privately, he put his fingers into his ears, and after spitting touched his tongue. And looking up to heaven, he sighed and said to him, "Ephphata," that is, "Be opened." And his ears were opened, his tongue was released, and he spoke plainly. And Jesus charged them to tell no one. But the more he charged them, the more zealously they proclaimed it. And they were astonished beyond measure, saying, "He has done all things well. He even makes the deaf hear and the mute speak." (Mark 7:31-37, ESV)

When you reveal yourself to people, you really need to be in front of someone who loves you. It isn't the time to be around people who don't care for you, is it? Revealing self was the experience of this mute, deaf man.

Often mistreated, cast aside, and ignored, he was used to people looking over him and treating him as if he was meaningless, useless, and inhumane. Everyone didn't look at him in those ways. There were people begging Jesus to lay hands on the man. That said, people in his day were like people in ours, often undervaluing others with different abilities or undervaluing persons with disabilities. Lump your tendency or my practice of acting as if older people or children or uneducated people or poor people aren't worthy, and we'll be close to the persons this man experienced. He knew something about being seen differently and being treated differently.

When friends brought him to Jesus, I imagine him wondering whether those folks were setting him up to be a punch line to a joke. You probably shouldn't read this passage without wondering to yourself how often you treat people as if they weren't created in the same God-image as you've been. I probably need to ask regularly whether I am, by my life, truly bringing people into the presence of Jesus for healing. Am I doing something else? Are you doing something else? Is that person on the ridiculed end of a joke? If that was this man's internal wondering, it wasn't because he didn't know something about ridicule.

Still, I'd like to focus on Jesus' gesture rather than the people's effort, even though their efforts were honorable. Rather than looking at their motive, consider Jesus. Jesus took this mistreated man to the side, pulled him into a private place, and ministered to him. Notice that the One who is able to heal was able to do it in a way that was affirming and honoring. Jesus healed this man, and he did something else we might easily miss: he respected him. Jesus' act of pulling him to the side to work with him, to touch him, and to speak to him communicated respect. This was love on display.

Jesus still works this way. He still works around a person's intimate issues. If it's hearing, seeing or speaking that's your issue, Jesus doesn't abuse you in order to heal you. If we have a vision of his diagnostic practice in this text, Jesus skillfully gathers what he needs when he takes the man away from the crowd.

There are some parts of your story that are between you and Jesus. If they are shared, it's not him who shares them. Some matters he keeps between you and him. Isn't that wonderful? He won't broadcast the words you speak. He won't tell others about your stammering when, in disbelief, you state your first words.

Jesus doesn't perform his miracles in a boastful way. He doesn't love your pained places in embarrassing ways. You may be pained by a family problem, an addiction to something unseen, by a series of dreams, by a breakup, or by a hope. Whatever your pain, in healing you, Jesus still loves you. Another way of saying that is that Jesus loves you all the way through your healing. In touching this man, Jesus acted in love. From beginning to ending, he does the same when he works for your healing.

Guiding Questions

1. How have you understood healing as part of your discipleship?
2. Have you ever been healed in a painful part of your soul?
3. What healing have you prayed for recently?

One Next Step

Claim your healing. By that I mean name your healing as a part of your life as a follower of Jesus. You can do this by facing the things that plague you and calling Jesus to attend to those things. You need not turn away from them or act as if they aren't real. Pain is a direct way for Jesus to work, a specific way for God to expand God's work in you. Name the places that wound you because they are the very places and parts of you that will provide you with daily evidence of the presence of the Healer.

Prayer

Lord, grant that I might live this way, touching, reaching, talking to, and holding onto all your people, especially sick and mistreated people. Make me respectful and, therefore, like Jesus. And open me to me. Show me the pained places in my soul. Where I've quieted my desires. Where I've been so wounded that I've ceased to speak. Take me to the side. Begin to heal me. Continue to heal me. Amen.

Blessing

All my pains are in Jesus' hands this week.
All my pains are held by the One who heals.

Faith for a Future

In those days, when again a great crowd had gathered, and they had nothing to eat, he called his disciples to him and said to them, "I have compassion on the crowd, because they have been with me now three days and have nothing to eat. And if I send them away hungry to their homes, they will faint on the way. And some of them have come from far away." And his disciples answered him, "How can one feed these people with bread here in this desolate place?" And he asked them, "How many loaves do you have?" They said, "Seven." And he directed the crowd to sit down on the ground. And he took the seven loaves, and having given thanks, he broke them and gave them to his disciples to set before the people; and they set them before the crowd. And they had a few small fish. And having blessed them, he said that these also should be set before them. And they ate and were satisfied. And they took up the broken pieces left over, seven baskets full. And there were about four thousand people. And he sent them away. And immediately he got into the boat with his disciples and went to the district of Dalmanutha. (Mark 8:1-10, ESV)

This passage is the bracket to the earlier miracle in Mark 6. In both passages Jesus is doing many things worth noticing, many things worth imitating. It's also worth noticing the proximity between the earlier miracle—of which the disciples were a part—and this one, leaving us to wonder why the disciples had questions about which Jesus so recently demonstrated answers. They were in Mark 6, yet in this chapter, they questioned his ability to feed a crowd. Nonetheless, their memory and forgetfulness become an occasion for us to consider our own memories.

    They lost sight of the recent things Jesus did. Taking the text at face value, they had experienced Jesus feeding people days ago, and they still questioned him in the desolate place. Of course, it could have been many days between the feedings, but how do you forget seeing Jesus miraculously feed thousands? It was as if their previous encounter hadn't happened—whenever it did. It was as if Jesus had changed into a different person, as if they had changed into different people who could no longer recall the rich feeling of a satisfied stomach at that first event. There are meals you forget and meals you don't. Somehow, they forgot.

    Can you relate to them? When it comes to the non-miraculous, it takes discipline to recall what God has done in your midst. So much happens to you daily, and you forget most of it. Take the last day and try to remember everything that happened at any random hour. Try it. Test yourself. You can't remember everything that happened from 11am to noon. Sure, you'll remember a meeting that was on your calendar. You'll remember that you went to the gas station. But will you recall how you got to the station, what route you took, and the color of the car that was ahead of you in the line at the pump?

Adding God into it, noticing God's activity in your life, makes memory even more complicated. It's hard. It's easy to forget. Big things (and who evaluates whether God's gesture is big or small?) and small things come and go from our memories. That's where community can help. In this scriptural case, it doesn't seem to help, but in general, people help other people remember. Knowing the past is what people do together. For instance, the church remembers its past and as a community does what no one person can do. In a fundamental sense, the faith community is a remembering community. When you forget what God does, corporate prayer times with your church bring before you those very acts.

Make an effort to give your memory to God regularly. You can do this by reviewing your days to "capture" a conversation, a reading, an impression, or a "feeding" that you know came from Jesus. Memory can become a means of you experiencing grace daily. It can be a means to you believing in God's accomplishments in the past. A grace-filled memory can be the means through which you nurture faith for the future. In a sense, it's silly to ask with the disciples, "How will this be done?" when you've already seen the answer. Perhaps bolstering your memory will aid you in answering your own question. And when you can't recall what's happened, draw upon the resource of someone else's memory. God gives others the memories you don't have so that, in community, you feed your faith for the future.

Guiding Questions

1. How do you define a miracle?
2. Thinking about the distance you've traveled with Jesus, how far have you come?
3. What helps you keep and celebrate your memories with God?

One Next Step

Review your day. Think back over the last 24 hours. Notice what happened. There will be things God allows you to notice, things you didn't pay much attention to when they happened. Then, after noticing what happened, step through those events. Where was God especially active? Where was God less active? You might pray over those moments. You might notice how it felt revisiting those events. You can also do this as a weekly exercise. If it's something you're drawn to, investigate the Prayer of Examen, and implement it as part of your spiritual practice.

Prayer

I will not forget the things you've done.
I will not let my mind release the blessings you've given.
I will remember what you've done for me.
I will remember, with others, all your works.
Together we will praise you.
These are my expectations for us.

Empower us with the grace to accomplish them.
Bless me and bless us with the God-kissed memory to recall all you've done.
Amen.

Blessing

My mind is a source of faith and I will use my best mind to strengthen my trust in God.

Hearing with Gentle Ears

And he said to them, "Do you not yet understand?" (Mark 8:21, ESV).

In any other person's mouth this question can undo you. "Don't you get it? What's wrong with you? Why can't you just...?" Part of the reason these kinds of questions can undo you is because of how subtle (and perhaps easy) it is to give others power over you, power to change your moods, power to make you feel like you're unworthy. Part of the undoing is because you might give the *wrong* people such power.

Granting authority—the ability for someone to author aspects of your story—is a gift. Everyone shouldn't be given that gift. Some people misuse authority. Consider whether you give Jesus the authority to tell you who you are, the right to question you, and the space to provide the context for your soul's best conversations. There is a way to hear Jesus' questions. And it's with gentle ears.

Hearing with gentle ears is not hearing Jesus as if he's screaming or as if his voice is exhausted by telling you the same thing over and over. Jesus doesn't have to raise his voice. In fact, his voice sets the sound of all voices. His tone, unlike your own when you're frustrated, is full of peace. His tone is, always, gentle. Jesus is not like me as I was trying to show my son how to write a capital "K" when he was first introduced to writing. I was frustrated and waiting for a real teacher. Since preschool, Bryce has gotten a lot better with his penmanship. His letters look great when he takes his time. They are very different from when he first started writing. I have gotten a lot better too, working with him more patiently and more often on his homework.

Before, I was angry having to learn how to teach him, having to learn how to come alongside our first son when he was learning what all those pencils did and how all those lines connected to make letters. At that time, Jesus' voice sounded more like my wife's voice when she was explaining the same. There was a softness that was as clear as it was encouraging. There was ability in her tone; she possessed encouragement and assurance. There was gentleness, and through her speaking, she taught our boy how to hear with gentle ears. I taught him things but hearing with gentle ears wasn't one of my early lessons.

It takes work to hear with gentle ears, especially when you're used to believing that Jesus has bad things to say to you and about you. It may feel impossible to believe that Jesus can speak or question you kindly. I don't know what you have the most trouble with when it comes to hearing with gentleness. You may have to get over the plaguing, unsettling feeling of being examined, of being inspected, and of coming up short. You may have to hear past voices of people in your family of origin. You may have to listen beyond the persons at your work or in your school or, even, in your church. It takes faith to keep listening and it takes courage to hear with kindness.

Take Jesus' method and way to heart, and trust that the questions Jesus asks are gentler. In them you are being examined and encouraged, tested and taught not only some specific point but also how to be gentle. His questions both illuminate your ignorance and expose you to truth about gentleness. After all, *he* is asking you. He speaks in the spirit of gentleness and, at the same time, in the spirit of truth.

Guiding Questions

1. What is the kindest thing God has ever said to you?
2. How might you challenge yourself to attend to the kind messages of the scriptures?
3. Who has wounded you by the things they've said?

One Next Step

Notice the impact of words on your life. Take a few minutes of quiet to consider phrases that always make you feel bad about yourself. Jot them down and see if you can come up with the story behind those phrases. Who first used them against you? Who do you think of when you re-read them? What happens inside when those words are spoken to you? After spending some time researching through those questions, ask the Holy Spirit to let you hear God's response to the phrases. Perhaps there are scriptures or other texts which come to mind to stand next to those phrases. Perhaps something God says contradicts what others have said. Notice the power of those earlier words and the power of God's words to help you in your becoming gentle.

Prayer

There are certainly things I don't understand. I beat myself up about those things rather than come to you, my Teacher. Humble me and remind me that my help comes from you. Collect the questions I've left unanswered.

Then, walk me through new lessons. Expose me to your latest classrooms. Counsel me through every long course. Allow my soul to blossom under your instruction. Grow me, teach me, and fortify me.
Amen.

Blessing

Not only I am able to speak blessings to others, I am also able to hear those blessings spoken over me. I will hear with gentle ears. I will attune myself to kindness.

Understanding Takes Time

They went on from there and passed through Galilee. And he did not want anyone to know, for he was teaching his disciples, saying to them, "The Son of Man is going to be delivered into the hands of men, and they will kill him. And when he is killed, after three days he will rise." But they did not understand the saying, and were afraid to ask him. (Mark 9:30-32, ESV)

Jesus saw his death coming, and he lovingly warned his followers. He warned them of what was to come. Of course, he knew of more than his approaching death. He knew he was investing in his group of followers. He knew that they were slowly taking up his teachings and that they were patterning themselves after his Father's kingdom. Still, Jesus saw the event of his dying, and he had to share what he saw. What a leader!

I think of him being extremely generous in opening his soul to his friends. He could have kept such information to himself. After all, these people did care about Jesus. Why tell them he was going to die?

The longer I work as a chaplain the more I see these kinds of conversations as acts of love. When a person plans for death, sees her life ending, talking about that eventual end is a very loving act. To tell one's family what your wishes are for your medical care, what your hopes are for the care of your body after death, and how you'd like to be remembered are intentional acts of seeing death and respecting death. They are also intentional acts of seeing and respecting the life you've lived. Finally, those conversations mark the meaning others have had in your life. It's loving to have the kinds of conversations that Jesus sparks.

When I think about this story and these disciples, I'm not sure if the rendering of this conversation is good enough. On a personal level, if a teacher of mine was about to die, or if a friend of mine saw death coming, or if someone I loved had to relay this news, they'd have to do *a lot* better than tell me in third person. No titles for me, Son of Man. Use your nickname or mine, tell me straight, and I'll have to hear it. We'd both be pressed to do what needed to be done.

Maybe Mark didn't want to admit it, years later, as these records were compiled. Maybe it was too much, to re-see death coming with its companion, grief. Jesus started saying these strange things after Peter made an equally strange claim, "You are the Christ." One bold claim traded with another. Jesus began to respond to Peter's proclamation with, "I'm dying soon."

Perhaps you've heard words like those from the lips of a loved one. Maybe you've sat vigil at the bedside of someone dying. Perhaps you sat with the face of a student in view as she told you her plans after graduation, plans that meant severing ties with family or friends. Maybe you held someone's hand when they tried to tell you a secret that tortured them because it meant mourning. You have your own experience with bold claims.

All these and other instances repeat something from the depths of humanity. They are versions of revelations like "You are the Christ" or "I'm dying soon." Of course, Jesus offered these grievous words to his disciples. In your life, you've heard them in your own setting.

They carry deep meanings. They are dying declarations, in a sense, words uttered by people who see the end coming. Those words are clear and pressed from all sides by truth. Disorienting and potent, such utterances change you. They make you hear and see and live differently. They unhinge you.

To understand those declarations, to understand the grief of a soon-departing Jesus is to start a whole new life. Understanding takes a long time. Forty days of Lent. An entire life. All eternity.

Will we ever understand the death of this man? Will we ever? To be a disciple is to move toward understanding. It is to walk in the pattern of this person who could say such things to his close friends and know that they would get it eventually.

Guiding Questions

1. Can you relate to the conversation between Jesus and the disciples?
2. What significance does Jesus' death have in your spiritual life?
3. How might you talk to your loved ones about life and about death?

One Next Step

Look over the Gospel of Mark for a word or phrase from Jesus that speaks to you. Hold onto that phrase this week. Turn it over. Place it upon your lips during moments of difficulty. Listen to what Jesus said in that phrase. Ask God to let you exhaust those words for the week you're living. Ask God to grant you more understanding.

Prayer

My life and my death are in your hands. That's always been true, even though it's hard to accept. Grant me the grace to see every future, imminent and eternal. Let me accept the beauty and the mystery which come with those tomorrows. Banish fear from my sight and help see beyond now. Give me daily light for the step in front of me. Amen.

Blessing

I can accept each eventual ending.
I can handle it when it comes.
I can love through every step.

Ask Different Questions

And they came to Capernaum. And when he was in the house he asked them, "What were you discussing on the way?" But they kept silent, for on the way they had argued with one another about who was the greatest. And he sat down and called the twelve. And he said to them, "If anyone would be first, he must be last of all and servant of all." And he took a child and put him in the midst of them, and taking him in his arms, he said to them, "Whoever receives one such child in my name receives me, and whoever receives me, receives not me but him who sent me." (Mark 9:33-37, ESV)

I've begun to see the practice of silence as a practice that can include saying only essential things and as a way of listening more than before. In general, I think it's a good practice to say less. I can talk all day. I have a thought or an opinion about anything! I'm not chatty by any means, but I'm pretty opinionated, if you ask.

Related to that, I get caught up in all kinds of meaningless conversation, all kinds of chatter. Like the disciples coming from Capernaum, I question whether I'm this or that, and eventually I find that I've been headed in the wrong verbal direction all along. I've been curious, genuinely interested in something, but that thing leads me further from the truth about myself. I'm, in a word, prideful.

Humility comes with different questions. It emerges as I seek to live into the words of Jesus about putting a child in the center of the room and learning from the child. In the time of Jesus, children were at the bottom of the social ladder. They were the last ones to consider. In fact, no one generally considered them—and Jesus began to say in his way, "Live like children." To live or approach life like children meant more than to be a good parent who was kind and compassionate. It meant to fundamentally reorient yourself and how you evaluated your life. Receiving a child in the name of Jesus meant being hospitable to people who were overlooked entirely by every system in the known world.

Jesus was calling for his followers to ask different questions. He was calling for them to ask whether or not they've been low enough in the world, close enough to the realities of everyone, including the uncounted of society. They had been arguing about greatness, asking about who fit better in the apostolic and discipling community. They had been back and forth about their qualities and how they were best suited for the spots closest to Jesus. They spoke about greatness, and Jesus responded that their topics and their questions were restricted to their small views of the world. All those words and they weren't really talking about what mattered.

Jesus invited them to see themselves differently. He invited them to the hard task of seeing the world in a new way. It would take courage and boldness. It would take heart to accept that their views of greatness were misdirected and that their views of self were, too. It would take courage to see that their understanding of children and everybody else needed to change.

In a world where children have "nothing to say," that act immediately expresses what a person thinks about themselves. When a person learns from the *unqualified*, they've begun to be humble. They've begun to learn. You can draw from this biblical context. Who will be your teachers today? Jesus tells you the result: you will, in receiving children, receive him. What a gift! Receiving Jesus, taking in Jesus, accepting in deep ways the God who accepts you. What can be better?

This offering of Jesus is beyond changing how you see yourself. It's about how you see yourself in relation to everyone else. Accept this challenge to ask new questions and to, in that asking, enter further the kingdom of God.

Guiding Questions

1. Who will be your teachers today?
2. What questions are you working with in the presence of God?
3. What do you want to learn this year?

One Next Step

Take a course about something that'll help you grow. It may be a language class, a pottery workshop or a martial arts class. It may be at your church or it may be far from your church. It may not be anything explicitly spiritual. Let your guideline be growth. Look for an experience that will help you grow and deepen a part of your life that needs attention. As you get into the class, even if it isn't this week, notice how God uses the material to engage you in the loving work of being new.

Prayer

You love children.
In your love for children, you show me that everyone is loved. Help me to extend myself in every loving way. Help me to be a lover after your kind, giving and accepting. Grant me the power of soul to notice my wrong questions. Give me the courage to face my ignorance. Enable me to follow a graced path toward new knowing and new being. I will follow you until I change. I will follow you as I change. I will follow you. Amen.

Blessing

I am surrounded by people who are worth loving.
We are all worth loving, worth respecting.

Tending to Your Path

As he was starting out on a trip, a man came running up to Jesus, knelt down, and asked, Good Teacher, what should I do to get eternal life?" "Why do you call me good?" Jesus asked. "Only God is truly good. But as for your question, you know the commandments: 'Do not murder. Do not commit adultery. Do not steal. Do not testify falsely. Do not cheat. Honor your father and mother.'" "Teacher," the man replied, "I've obeyed all these commandments since I was a child." Jesus felt genuine love for this man as he looked at him. "You lack only one thing," he told him. "Go and sell all you have and give the money to the poor, and you will have treasure in heaven. Then, come, follow me." (Mark 10:17-21, NLT)

Jesus used metaphors when talking about the relationship between God and the world. He spoke of people and jobs, animals and food. He was a teacher who called upon every literary resource that his listeners could appreciate. Like a good cook, he prepared his teachings as if they were meals, and he pulled together nourishing ingredients. He would offer what he had to people like the man in this passage. This person wanted to know what to do to grow, and he came to Jesus, the one everyone suggested could answer his abiding question.

I hear in his question about eternal life a strong desire for goodness, a God-given ache for wholeness, even if that ache is covered over by intellect, self-assurance, and a propensity to categorize what can't be categorized. Jesus disrupts this man in a way that opens him. He doesn't sit within the confines of this questioner's categories. Jesus begins to open up a truth that there is no recipe for spiritual growth, no list of ingredients that, when meticulously measured, blended, and heated, can combine to nourish and lengthen you for the kingdom of God.

God's kingdom involves people who are diverse and (at least to us) unpredictable. Instead of exact replicas that look alike, in kingdom life hundreds of recipes blend for the new creation that emerges. Countless metaphors snatch at the great and bold work of God, and the baking, rising, and setting of what, in God's kingdom, awaits you and your discovery. Your path opens for you to find your language, your metaphor, and your specific way of growing.

Now, this has been true for all of human history. The paths before you are yours but they have the prints of people who have walked down similar spiritual roads. That is to say that there are practices that bring you before God, which make you honest and show you mirrors in the Presence; those mirrors and paths have the smudges and prints of your forebears. Like them, you hear truth carefully offered.

You try to pray. You serve. You breathe. In the words of the man questioning Jesus, you "obey those commands." They are clear and you go forward with them.

Those moments of clarity are when you see your real self, when you see more clearly who God is. Those moments are like seeds budding. And your ears open. Your darkness diminishes. That is the impact upon following the paths on which God places your feet, obeying the commands that God makes so clear. The brightness comes, and it's meant to be shared.

The brightness is meant to be given away because light is good at exposing darkness. Can you think of a part of you that's locked in darkness? It may be a way to stay on your path—a way to tend to your own soul—a way to find wisdom and guidance in the old, common path of these commands. When you're uncertain of how to live in the light, you can return to the basics found on those paths, the ones with the prints of your forebears.

They're negatively worded: not murdering, not committing adultery, not stealing. Those negative efforts (not doing certain things) provide you with clear direction when it's hard to get to clarity. They don't compose a recipe for growth, but they are specific and diverse ways to stay faithful.

They are ways to remain clear about some things when many things feel uncertain. Those old, used commands are a way to stay faithful when you need a way to stay faithful. They come in handy when everything else is in question form. They are statements, unquestionably given as markers in the direction of life.

Guiding Questions

1. How do you incorporate the commandments into your life?
2. What do you find Jesus telling you these days?
3. When has your faithfulness been rewarded and when has it been frustrated?

One Next Step

Have a conversation with a friend, one you haven't seen in a while. Try to leave your motives aside, be open to the meeting, and be open to what occurs. Pay attention to what you hear. You may be surprised at what comes up. That conversation—just by having it—may be a space of grace and benefit. There may also be something worth hearing about how you move forward from it.

Prayer

I want to obey you, yet, I often don't.
I stray when I intend to stay.
I falter when I hope to commit.
Something in me desires to follow hard.
And the competing motive is present, too.
I want two things: to follow and to flee.
Strengthen the parts of me that desire to follow.
Be gentle and firm with those that don't.
Tell me more about those parts that want to flee.
In knowing them, I'll get in touch with your stable grace.
Amen.

Blessing

Everything I do has the potential to bring me closer to Jesus who loves me.

I will think carefully today, knowing that my choices have power.

Think of Them

Jesus said, "Truly, I say to you, there is no one who has left house or brothers or sisters or mother or father or children or lands, for my sake and for the gospel, who will not receive a hundredfold now in this time, houses and brothers and sisters and mothers and children and lands, with persecutions, and in the age to come eternal life. But many who are first will be last, and the last first. (Mark 10:29-31, ESV)

    Think of this. Everything you've lost returning. Every love you've left coming back eternally. That includes deep friendships that were taken, snatched, and never allowed to end well. Conversations which were completely interrupted continuing. The bruises of deaths being healed by unending and sweet reunions. The tortures of closed caskets trading with open smiles and long hugs and the press of lips from kisses you never want to stop.

    A table spread with all your favorite foods, lined or circled with chairs for every special person you ever knew, with settings of special plates and candles and appetizers you know that they'll love. Soundtracks with your favorite songs playing except the songs you sang when your heart was broken even though you know they were the real lyrics of all those days of grief.

Distance increasing between you and the dark, you and the pain, you and the realness of life before eternity. All these matters of your heart coming before the bliss and the terrible purity of perfect, enduring Love. These are too sentimental to be the precise meaning of the Savior's words. But they are in my imagination when I read these words slowly. What's in yours? What might this eternal life look like?

Jesus did not focus on the age to come. His ministry to those who followed was largely about their lives in the present age. He spoke about life in the next age—his words mattered for life then, too, of course—but his emphases were around the relationships people were in at the time. He fed people who were hungry after his sermon. He saved people from the anxiety of sickness and the raging waters after fishing for a day. He healed fevers and ailments. He raised people from death. Those expressions were about the present and not the future.

Still, there was no false choice with Jesus. He gave attention to now *and* later. There was the healing in the moment *and* the proclamation of a splendid future where his followers would "receive a hundredfold." Living as if both are true takes effort. You probably lean toward one or the other, inclining toward the right now aspects of life or toward the long season of your tomorrows. Living in the now would mean focusing on what's here. Living in the future would mean focusing on what's not yet. Jesus taught that both mattered.

They are meant to relate, meant to be in tension or, I prefer, meant to dance. Believing Jesus here takes courage. Following him as if this dance is true takes grace. And there is blessing in believing, blessing in living as if these words are real. He says that you will receive. Yes, you've lost and gone without and been recipient to harsh wounds or pain. There is no one who has experienced these things who will not "receive a hundredfold."

In the kingdom that Jesus loves, there is a reward for your life. That reward does not remove the burdens of your life. Remember that Jesus spent his life at work in addressing those very burdens. He healed. He persisted. He also held up this future orientation in order to whet your visionary appetite for more. You have both available in the kingdom. Your life matters. Your beautiful life matters. It doesn't end when your breath ends so everything you place your hands upon has the potential to turn the world toward the significance of life. Imagine it continuing. Imagine those sweet reunions. Think of them.

Guiding Questions

1. What's in your imagination when you read the words of Jesus?
2. What might eternal life look like?
3. How is a vision of life beyond now a resource for your walk with God?

One Next Step

Spend some time this week thinking about what Jesus says. Consider who you've left and what you've lost. Your reflection may bring hints of old pain, echoes of past wounds. That remembering, in the presence of Jesus, can bring deep connection to the words of Jesus here. List those things you've given up. And then imagine what God will give you. Imagine what "a hundredfold" blessing might include in your case. You may see in your heart images from the Spirit, images that may help you get in touch with what it means to be first.

Prayer

Grant me the courage to believe what you say.
Help me sit with these words as long I've sat in my grief.
You can be trusted.
You can be believed.
You will replenish me.
You will heal me.
I will receive hundredfold.
I don't know what that means.
But I will trust that it's true.
I will live with open hands and open eyes.
I will live now and later as if Jesus would only tell the truth.
Amen.

Blessing

I have lost and may still lose, but I will trust Jesus still.

Refusing to Read

And they were on the road, going up to Jerusalem, and Jesus was walking ahead of them. And they were amazed, and those who followed were afraid. And taking the twelve again, he began to tell them what was to happen to him, saying, "See, we are going up to Jerusalem, and the Son of Man will be delivered over to the chief priests and the scribes, and they will condemn him to death and deliver him over to the Gentiles. And they will mock him and spit on him, and flog him and kill. And after three days he will rise. (Mark 10:32-34, ESV)

Does it get old to you, the description of his ministry? Can you pass by these words and not feel something in your throat, some conviction that it must be a lie, some hope even that it didn't happen this way?

When I'm at my best, I read Jesus' words here—where he is telling of his death beforehand—and I pause to thank God and to repent of my part in the shameful death of the Son. When I'm at my worst, and this is usually the case, I simply *read* these words, read them like they are other words.

I don't open myself up to an impact. I read them, get it done, and go on the next part. I go on the part about three days, realizing that we're living post-resurrection, explaining away his suffering as if it were fleeting. And in my refusing to read deeply, I diminish what's there.

Jesus is persistent with his disciples. He lays down these words of preparation, I think, so they aren't surprised, so that they have some inkling of a future when he'll be executed. He loves them so much, even while knowing that they don't fully get it. He still rehearses all the death in front of him, no doubt compounding his suffering. In a way, their corporate refusal to accept what he's told them about his death is your refusal and my refusal.

It's easy to leave deep readings of the scriptures to someone else. Perhaps your preacher should be the one reading deeply. Perhaps the person you trust with your soul should read deeply, even when you don't trust yourself with the same. A small group leader. A Sunday school teacher.

Jesus says to his first disciples what he says to you: the same old thing. Jesus offers the same message about suffering. "Expect it," he seems to say. Be accustomed to this. Suffering is coming. It will not destroy you but it's ahead. There is more on the other side of it. Do we really read what he's said? Do we know what Jesus has been saying all this time?

Yet, I wonder if I hear him and if you hear him. I wonder if we sit with these heavy, early warnings or if it's just easier to attend to what's in front at the moment. My son, Bryce, is great at attending to what's in front of him. He will take what's in your hand rather than wait for some unforeseen future gift. Even when the future gift is better, he'll accept what his eyes see now. The future isn't conceivable for him. Right now is. I get it because he's young. Still, Bryce helps me understand these disciples when it comes to hearing Jesus, reading Jesus, and accepting Jesus. Taking his words in requires courage; it takes age. Accepting that Jesus will die—has died, has lost—requires strength to accept the unthinkable, maturity to take it all in.

It requires the courage to say that your guy lost. Your God endured suffering and still got beat by it, even if for a while. It requires a long enough track record to see that the life coming from Jesus included a grand loss. That's incredible humility because as quickly as preachers preach over those days Jesus spent in the grave, he was still there. He still lay there dead.

Maybe it is easier to refuse that reality. Maybe it's easier to tell yourself, even if it happened, it isn't worth holding too tightly. But death is death. Dead is dead. When death is what you have, you can't get by it. Acceptance is the way. Surrender is the gesture.

Guiding Questions

1. What does it mean to be open to suffering?
2. How have you suffered in your life?
3. Where have you felt particularly surrendered in relationship to Jesus?

One Next Step

Accept the suffering in your life. Sit next to it. Own it. Call it yours. See the power in that, the power in accepting that the present suffering is actually present.

Why is that weak? When following Jesus, there's probably nothing stronger. Perhaps this week you can, by accepting what's in your life, build a new appreciation for your life.

Prayer

My suffering is real.
Do you see it?
My pains are sharp.
Can you sense them?
My grief stands and screams.
Are you hearing it?
My hopes left.
Have you found them?
My ambitions are bruised.
Can they be recovered?
I don't know what you'll say to my hardship.
But say something.
Speak to me the way you have to my forebears.
Speak.
Please.
Amen.

Blessing

My suffering makes me available for strength.
I will be stronger even if my suffering isn't worthy.
I will be stronger.

Downward Aspirations

And James and John, the sons of Zebedee, came up to him and said to him, "Teacher, we want you to do for us whatever we ask of you." And he said to them, "What do you want me to do for you?" And they said to him, "Grant us to sit, one at your right hand and one at your left, in your glory." Jesus said to them, "You do not know what you are asking. Are you able to drink the cup that I drink, or to be baptized with the baptism with which I am baptized?" And they said to him, "We are able." And Jesus said to them, "The cup that I drink you will drink, and the baptism with which I am baptized, you will be baptized, but to sit at my right hand or at my left is not mine to grant, but it is for those for whom it has been prepared." And when the ten heard it, they began to be indignant at James and John. And Jesus called them and said to them, "You know that those who are considered rulers of the Gentiles lord it over them, and their great ones exercise authority over them. But it shall not be so among you. But whoever would be great among you must be your servant, and whoever would be first among you must be slave of all. For even the Son of Man came not to be served but to serve, and to give his life as a ransom for many." (Mark 10:35-45, ESV)

Jesus doesn't question the desires of James and John. He questions the vision and knowledge underneath them. In other words, Jesus questions what they see about the seats they're claiming.

Their request is clear, and it's offensive to their disciple-friends who are listening to their bold hopes. They want something everyone wants, to be great. They want to sit near Jesus, to be near him. They want to rule with him. They want greatness. All good things. Jesus leaves their desires unquestioned. What he does question is how they achieve that greatness.

The work of James K.A. Smith helps me think about how humans are desiring beings. I'm summarizing him here, and Smith says that we aren't thinking beings only. We are love animals, thoughtful and desiring, according to Smith. In this text, Jesus doesn't quash the wants and sentiments of these bold disciples. He recognizes that desires run at the core of his friends. The same is true for you.

Jesus' recognition can help you see your own desires, especially if you're the type to turn away from wants and hopes for fear that they have inherent badness. There's nothing bad in wanting. For these two in the text, it doesn't even come up. The posture they seek, being in close proximity to the Lord in his glory, is admirable. Jesus only says that they don't understand the whole idea. They don't see the full picture because they're concentrating on glory. Jesus turns them to a different consideration. "Look lower," he seems to say.

I wonder if this is a rule of life for us: to look lower. To aspire for more terrestrial things; to push our eyes downward, toward the darkness, toward the humble, even if it goes against the good, easy human tendency toward grandeur; perhaps this is the rule to which life must be gauged. Jesus doesn't say, "Don't want." He seems to say, "Want another. Want lower. Want something of a different quality." It feels like a correction to me. I hear Jesus inviting you and me to consider the direction of our desires. Point them east rather than south, if you will.

Then, there is this notion that followers of Jesus can be great if they are willing to serve. This is the bottom of the barrel when compared to what the initial question seemed to be. John and James asked about reigning and the conversation ends with Jesus explaining service and sacrifice. He says that the first person among the disciples is the person who serves and who gives life away.

This isn't about saving the best seats, this sacrifice business. Jesus pushes his friends away from the topic of power and moves them to the real behavior of greatness. He shows them—certainly through his own actions—what greatness looks like: giving your life for something and someone else.

The wants weren't the issue here. Their direction was. Their orientation was the pivotal piece to greatness. In serving others, their own lives would not only be preserved but they would also take on increasing greatness. Jesus offers a path to life and a path to greatness in his conversation. It's inherent generosity, giving of oneself and, in that, giving to oneself.

Guiding Questions

1. How would you describe the direction of your desires?
2. What does Jesus' view of service mean to you?
3. What do you want?

One Next Step

Train your desires to be in step with Jesus. This is not entirely a work for God alone. You have a part to play. You can turn your hopes and wants in the direction that honors God. As you read this reflection, did your heart move in a particular direction? Did an image or person come to before you? Sit with that impression and see if there is a place to go or a direction in which to turn. See if you can attach your desire to it and, following closely, be in step with Jesus.

Prayer

I've wondered over this business of greatness.
I've been told, on one hand, that my people aren't great.
I've been told about my lack of this and my poverty in that.
I've wanted a different experience of the world.
I've wanted fullness.
I've wanted to reign.
But I'm listening to you, Jesus, and changing my view.
I still want things.
I still want more.

Give me a seat next to all the people who have no seats.
And in my sitting, may I notice you've been there too.

Blessing

I can give my life for something that matters.
I can be uncompromisingly great.

Disorienting Dilemmas

Now when they drew near to Jerusalem, to Bethphage and Bethany, at the Mount of Olives, Jesus sent two of his disciples and said to them, "Go into the village in front of you, and immediately as you enter it you will find a colt tied, on which no one has ever sat. Untie it and bring it. If anyone says to you, 'Why are you doing this?' say, 'The Lord has need of it and will send it back here immediately.'" And they went away and found a colt tied at a door outside in the street, and they untied it. And some of those standing there said to them, "What are you doing, untying the colt?" And they told them what Jesus had said, and they let them go. And they brought the colt to Jesus and threw their cloaks on it, and he sat on it. And many spread their cloaks on the road, and others spread leafy branches that they had cut from the fields. And those who went before and those who followed were shouting, "Hosanna! Blessed is he who comes in the name of the Lord! Blessed is the coming kingdom of our father David! Hosanna in the highest!" And he entered Jerusalem and went into the temple. And when he had looked around at everything, as it was already late, he went out to Bethany with the twelve. (Mark 11:1-11, ESV)

    Perspective transformation is a change to how you see something. One of the ways I've read through Mark is by being sensitive to Jesus as a leader in perspective transformation. One of his sweet spots is in illuminating how we see and how we might see. I've thought a lot about the power of perspective transformation. In my ministry in the church, I've found reframing to be a pretty nifty pastoral skill, and reframing is related to perspective transformation.

I'm currently in a certification process in clinical pastoral education, a part of my continuing education with some of these things. When I was getting consultation on a paper last year (as part of the process), one of the supervisors scribbled something down in the margin. This was at a meeting where I or a peer would generally present a paper or video of our practice and get immediate feedback. The engagement is great and laborious. As students, we get a massive amount of constructive, careful, and pointed critique from pastors who have been therapists, educators, and chaplains for years.

So, after my presentation, I brought my notes to the hospital and flipped through my friends' comments. I imagine that I also reviewed the event, almost writing a verbatim in my head about the presentation and the feedback in particular. Of course, the presentation came up in my own supervisory meeting with my training supervisor. One piece of feedback on my theological theory paper was to consider writing it as a meditation. This was what the supervisor I mentioned above scribbled. He knew I wrote devotionals and he asked me how my theory would come across if I looked at it similarly. "What if you wrote this as a meditation?"

He was offering me a potential perspective change. He used something I could relate to and employed it in what has become a change of my view. Not all changes of view are comfortable. And they always require work. But they can be gifts. They can be good gifts.

Look at Jesus in this text. He turns custom inside-out, upside-down. He mentions his identity as Creator, King, Lord and Son, and then he does *this*. He enters the city where he'll die, King that he is, with such meager acclaim. He's on a colt whose only underlined trait is its inexperience.

This is the way Jesus comes. He's not forceful; he's barely strong when facing the parade of cloaks and dung and dust. It feels like a stretch to call it regal. There he is approaching death and somehow still showing strength. That strength is covered with fortitude, steadiness, and contentment. It's covered with humility.

Always changing or challenging our perceptions and our expectations, Jesus comes on borrowed clothes and a borrowed animal. This is his way. This is his approach. Rather to his death, to the events subsequent to it, or to us, Jesus comes like this. This is the person who can change how you see.

Guiding Questions

1. What might this reflection mean for how Jesus enters your life this week?
2. How has God shown strength and how has God shown humility in your experience?

3. How do you define power?

One Next Step

Enter your next conversation after telling yourself that your identity is already sure. Before going into a meeting, talk to yourself from within your developing view of this humble, powerful Jesus. Tell yourself that you walk in step with him, that you can ride a stallion or that you can walk on your own feet. Remind yourself that whether people appraise you rightly or if they diminish you that God has found in your deep treasures.

Prayer

Show me what you've placed in me. Teach me how to value myself. Convince me by your words and not by the culture around me. Make sure I know how worthy and God-trusted I am. Help me hear what I need to and ignore what I need to. Straighten my gaze so that I look ahead and not aside. Embolden me by deepening me in who you've made me to be. Amen.

Blessing

I am humble to show strength not weakness.
I am humble to anchor in reality.
I am humble to know exactly who I am.
No more and no less.

The Power and Intimacy of Praying

As they passed by in the morning, they saw the fig tree withered away to its roots. And Peter remembered and said to him, "Rabbi, look! The fig tree that you cursed has withered." And Jesus answered them, "Have faith in God. Truly, I say to you, whoever says to this mountain, 'Be taken up and thrown into the sea,' and does not doubt in his heart, but believes that what he says will come to pass, it will be done for him. Therefore I tell you, whatever you ask in prayer, believe that you have received it, and it will be yours. And whenever you stand praying, forgive, if you have anything against anyone, so that your Father also who is in heaven may forgive you your trespasses." (Mark 11:20-26, ESV)

Figs were nutritious plants. If I were hungry in the time of Jesus and saw a fig tree appearing to have food, I'd expect food. I'd be upset, too! I wonder if Jesus even noticed the tree withering.

In my imagination, it took Peter to point this out because withering figs were natural to Jesus if he cursed the tree. Of course the tree would wither. I think Peter noticed something in his surprise that Jesus overlooked out of the depth of his relationship with his Father. I think Jesus had a faith that was worth aspiring to; I believe Peter is opening us to that aspiration.

This passage, and passages like it, has been abused to make prayer little more than sputtering desires and expecting each of them to come to us wrapped like gifts with big bows. But I think this passage provides a warning to be careful when praying, to take care when speaking in the ears of God. This passage is about how powerful what we say to God—and to others for that matter—is.

I don't think Jesus addresses doubt, though he isn't downplaying doubt. He says something about how doubt will impact the heart, how it will relate to the work of prayer, but he doesn't say that doubt is bad. This isn't a teaching about doubt. Rather, it's a teaching about asking God for what's in your heart. At a broader level, it's about talking to God based upon what's in your heart. If doubt is there, prayer at its best is a conversation between you and God about that doubt. Prayer is only prayer when it's communing with God about your real heart matters. That leads to the power inside of the practice of praying.

Prayer is intimate language. You're involved. The Spirit's involved. During prayer, you see what's in your life, what mountains are present. You take stock in what's concerning you. You're involved. Not some fake version of you but the real raw you. You are included in that soul work. Then, there's the Holy Spirit, the one who takes your prayers into the Divine Community and who brings the answers back. There is involvement from you and from the Spirit, and the math of prayer is amazing. The Spirit takes your words, digs into them for God's best promise, and offers those utterances to the Father for answering.

I think Jesus' words here should give you boldness and clarity. Boldness to come and say what you want, and clarity to inspect those wants as you ready yourself to pray. Your prayers will be answered by God. And it will be yours, says Jesus. That is a reason to pray and to expect that what you ask for will be answered. So, pray deeply and slowly and carefully knowing that what you want in your best self will come wrapped in love and grace.

Guiding Questions

1. When has your faith felt especially strong, especially weak?
2. What are you praying for these days?
3. How can this passage anchor your prayers?

One Next Step

Cultivating the intimacy between you and God means being vulnerable. A part of vulnerability is accepting what's happened, accepting when God has answered and accepting what questions still remain. Sit in quiet and think over your prayer life in recent weeks. Notice where you've felt heard by God and where you've felt unheard. Pay attention to your heart in each instance. Be vulnerable as the Spirit rests with you. As you consider your disappointments with God, ask the Spirit to settle you, to make you responsive to God's work, and to keep you open. Regard this time as prayer. You're deepening your walk with God.

Prayer

You've heard my prayers and I want to keep them before you. I want to remind you of my desires, point them out. I stand with these uplifted, each one on top of my faith. My hopes are in you. Don't let me down. Show that Jesus is right. Show that you're able. Amen.

Blessing

My life, as it is, is an opportunity for God to answer my heart's desires.

Getting Warm

And one of the scribes came up and heard them disputing with one another, and seeing that he answered them well, asked him, "Which commandment is the most important of all?" Jesus answered, "The most important is, 'Hear, O Israel: The Lord our God, the Lord is one. And you shall love the Lord your God with all your mind and with all your strength.' The second is this: 'You shall love your neighbor as yourself.' There is no other commandment greater than these." And the scribe said to him, "You are right, Teacher. You have truly said that he is one, and there is no other besides him. And to love him with all the heart and with the understanding and with all your strength, and to love one's neighbor as oneself, is much more than all whole burnt offerings and sacrifices." And when Jesus saw that he answered wisely, he said to him, "You are not far from the kingdom of God." And after that no one dared to ask him any more questions. (Mark 12:28-34, ESV)

I like Mark's rendering here of a scene that we've read in a couple places. This conversation ends with hopefulness. The scribe is not far. He's close. He's near the kingdom. Sometimes that's all you have—when you *want* to be in God's will. You desire what's truly good and best, and you hope that there's no difference between those two. You are near. You are in the neighborhood. You are close to the kingdom.

Scribes have well-considered positions, well-developed interpretations of sacred texts. At times, those well-conceived renderings, leave them (and you, perhaps) far away from the One who is the Center of all the sacred commands. Jesus says to the scribe, "You are not far." It's worth holding onto Jesus' words when he's says these things. It means that your efforts, your own hard thinking, and your considerations can play a part in getting you to receive what God brings. It's worth holding onto that you're near.

I'm sure that taking this line of thinking, about being near, is not the most common teaching point in faith communities. My own experience is that it's often more common to talk about the distance rather than the proximity. After all, pointing out how close you are to Jesus may leave you with less motivation to keep at it. If you hear like this man that you are not far from Jesus, perhaps you'll turn away, lose effort, or stop trying. That view is a poor one.

A richer view is to celebrate the distance you've traveled. A richer view is to see the long journey. A richer view is to notice exactly what Jesus is saying: look where you've come from and notice how you're near. When we would guess things as children, we'd say to the person guessing, "You're getting warm," when they were close to the answer. Getting cold meant the guess was going in the wrong direction. Getting hot meant they were really close. In the text, this man has gotten warm. He was warm and close. Talking about closeness to Jesus—rather than all the bad things you've done to bring distance between you and Jesus or all the differences between how you read the passage from how Jesus did—cultivates closeness.

This man wanted to engage Jesus. Perhaps he had other intentions. The text as written could mean that this scribe was a part of the contentious group who only wanted a dispute. The text could also be interpreted as if this man wanted to stand outside of that contentious group. He talked with Jesus, and after their conversation, no one else asked the same question. They had evidence of what was possible. The man's life testified to the possibility of being with Jesus and not, simply, against Jesus. In other words, they could be in the kingdom. Scribes, foes, and people who thought differently could be close to the kingdom. And closeness could get them something.

This is true for you. If you don't fall in line with everyone else's thinking, that doesn't mean you're distant. Perhaps you are closer to Jesus than you think. Perhaps you always have been.

Guiding Questions

1. How do you feel when you disagree with Jesus?
2. What can this exchange teach you about the kingdom?
3. What does it mean for *you* to love *your* neighbor?

One Next Step

Think about a time when you had no faith, when your hope was lost, when you thought you were far from Jesus. Take a piece of paper and write down on one side of it all the ways you felt far from Jesus. Then, re-read the gospel passage above. Revisit your list, and on the other side of the paper, imagine when and how you may have been close to Jesus, near to his kingdom during that same time. Write those down on that other side of the paper. Notice the first side. Celebrate the second side.

Prayer

Make me aware of the possibilities in my life.
Equip me with soul radar that keeps me open to them.
I want to see what you can do.
In me, in others, in the world.
Expand my view and stay out of my boxes for you.
You never fit boxes because you're always bigger.
You are what's possible.
I'm glad.
Amen.

Blessing

I am near to God.
I am in the mind of God.
I am in the will of God.
I am close to God.

Self-Examination

And in his teaching he said, "Beware of the scribes, who like to walk around in long robes and like greetings in the marketplaces and have the best seats in the synagogues and the places of honor at feasts, who devour widows' houses and for a pretense make long prayers. They will receive the greater condemnation." (Mark 12:38-40, ESV)

It's one thing to assume that Jesus is talking about someone else in this passage. It's another thing to own that he's speaking to you. When I read scriptures about the religious leaders in Jesus' time, for instance, I find myself thinking what I'd never do and how I'd never belong to this or that group. But when I think those thoughts, my reaction is false. A truer reaction seems to be in my seeing how I'm *already* like these people or that group, how I'm already included in the very ones that I think Jesus is talking against.

If I'm already in the group of those Jesus says to beware of, that means I need to approach God in a particular way. In a humble way. In a tentative way. In a way that's less self-assured. In a way that has less self-righteousness. That doesn't mean that I can't own my strength, but it does mean that I have to own my weaknesses, too.

Try not to consider *if* this text describes you when you pray but in what ways it *does*. The words of Jesus are here to help you discover your soul and uncover who you really are, even if the picture is not positive. In a firm way, the picture of who you really are is the only thing worth seeing. The composite that you've made up isn't worth seeing. It's not the real you.

What's worth seeing is who you are under your attempts to distance yourself from reality. I hope this is clear and gentle: you're not who you think you are. You're not who you pretend to be. You're probably very much who you're running from. That's the person that Jesus is trying to disciple, the person you're pretending you aren't.

The person whose pride swells. The person with that dreadful soul passenger that never leaves. The one with a deadly part of himself that you've worked hard not to let out, show up, or speak. That is the person that Jesus is coming for. In other words, you've already become the scribe praying long prayers. You've already been party to your own condemnation.

This text intends to awaken you to who you are and to give you an alternative. You who made a performance of yourself. You who lost the power that comes when you meet God. You who traded kingdom life for a life of people's praise. Jesus wants you. Jesus offers you more than a warning.

Jesus brings a way out of being the same as you've always been. Jesus gives you the strength to see who you've been and to accept that and the way to be different once you know who you've been. Jesus gives you the courage through the process of soul reclamation and change.

You don't need everything about you to change. There are stable, God-anchored elements to you that will not change. But the Spirit will upset those parts of you that lag behind in your walk with Jesus. The Spirit will show you where you need to grow. You can't grow without changing. You can't change with grace. And the grace you need is in God's hands; that grace is placed in your heart. Take advantage of God's grace by accepting it and letting it thrill the good work of the Spirit inside.

Guiding Questions

1. What might God be making in you?
2. How do you know when you've become complacent?
3. Why haven't you changed?

One Next Step

Write a list of changes you know you need to make but that you've resisted. It's a list, nothing to commit to, just something to prepare. Put on your list any change that you don't question you need. It only has to be a change that you cannot make. You know it's necessary and you know you haven't done it. When you're finished writing your list, read it, and then offer to God as a prayer. Tell God, in your own words, what your job is when it comes to the list and how you don't want to do that job. And sit in quiet. See if God has a response.

Prayer

I've worked hard to be the opposite of who I am. I thought I needed to be somebody else. I thought being different was required. Deep down I want to be whole, but I've covered up who I am in that pursuit. In covering up myself, I've become who I feared. And even then, you've loved me. Help me accept that reality. Help me accept love. Amen.

Blessing

There's nothing I can do to earn God's love
Because I have always been loved exactly as I am.
I live with that echoing in my bones.
I live with love as my music.

Contemplating Death

And as he sat on the Mount of Olives opposite the temple, Peter and James and John and Andrew asked him privately, "Tell us, when will these things be, and what will be the sign when all these things are about to be accomplished?" And Jesus began to say to them, "See that no one leads you astray. Many will come in my name, saying, 'I am he!' and they will lead many astray. (Mark 13:3-6, ESV)

Jesus starts a long answer that I've only offered a part of. He's discussing when the stones of the great buildings on the Temple grounds will be thrown down. All their surroundings, explains Jesus, will be changed. And his disciples are asking for a timeline and for an indication of when these things will happen.

In answering, Jesus asserts a few instructions that we do well to remember. The first is to be led well. I imagine that Jesus, as leader of that band of diverse and nutty students, feels many mixed feelings. He's facing his death. As he tells them about the future of their setting, the future of their lives, he's also looking through what is to come for himself. He's likely thinking about their conversations over those years. They spent many days together. Three years of living and serving together rested between them. Jesus would have seen this as a serious matter. And they, too probably felt in their bellies the swell of grief rising. They loved each other, cared for each other, and had spent their days being faithful in mission together.

Nobody's contemplation of death is without complexity. Death is an enemy and a friend. It feels foreign and it feels natural. Death brings grief. It brings rest and relief. It's complicated, especially when you have the luxury of considering yours before it happens. Death was what Jesus had prepared his followers for, his own death that is, and in preparing them for his death, Jesus was also equipping them for all the future deaths ahead.

I think Jesus left little reminders for his disciples on his way to that gross and ugly cross. There were strong reminders of who he was and what his kingdom was and how it was present and not present. There were reminders of how they ought to be without him. He said that they ought to be led well while they, like him, were dying. He told them to stay faithful.

He seems to be saying to them, as much as to himself, that their path would be sure and that whoever led them along that path should be faced in the same dismal direction. He seemed to say that all who helped his followers "endure" and "be saved" had led well.

This means that following Jesus, for you and not just them, is about following him all the way. Being led by Jesus is, in part, being led to your death. Wonderful Christian thinking has illuminated how following Jesus to death is both physical and spiritual. It is an actual death that you will meet, and it's not only the physical death. Deaths will come in many ways, sizes, and experiences. In all of these, Jesus offers a way for you to be led well.

So, as you think of following and of dying, be led today. Then, turn around to lead others well. Lead others toward death, in the sense of discipleship, so that they may see a choice in following this One who lived a life of prophetic service for God and the world. May God grant you the privilege.

Guiding Questions

1. What image comes to mind when you think about this scene at the table?
2. How does this language about contemplating death strike you?
3. What is leadership in your experience?

One Next Step

Consider the readying reminders of death that Jesus has provided for you, in particular, the small deaths leading to your character formation. Notice the signs in you showing that Jesus has been at work. Notice things in you that are dying or things in you that are changing. You may see a change in appetite. Perhaps you desire something you never noticed before. As a step in the direction of that area's death, commit to change one thing this week. Ask for grace from the Holy Spirit and act in a way consistent with the Spirit's provision. Be changed by grace.

Prayer

Teach me how to descend into death. Show me the way to follow Jesus in that steep decline. I have known death to bring fear, hopelessness, and despair. But I have also known Jesus. I want to know him in relation to death. I want to know death in relation to him. I want to see death differently because he conquered it. Lead me well in following him. Amen.

Blessing

When I die—during all my deaths—I will be surrounded by the loving example of a victorious Jesus.

Thank You

And while he was at Bethany in the house of Simon the leper, as he was reclining at table, a woman came with an alabaster flask of ointment of pure nard, very costly, and she broke the flask and poured it over his head. There were some who said to themselves indignantly, "Why was the ointment wasted like that? For this ointment could have been sold for more than three hundred denarii and given to the poor." And they scolded her. But Jesus said, "Leave her alone. Why do you trouble her? She has done a beautiful thing to me. For you always have the poor with you, and whenever you want, you can do good for them. But you will not always have me. She has done what she could; she has anointed my body beforehand for burial. And truly, I say to you, wherever the gospel is proclaimed in the whole world, what she has done will be told in memory of her." (Mark 14:3-9, ESV)

I think we've made Jesus out to be a liar. I can't think of the last time I heard a serious proclamation about you. But here's to recommending a fresh look at the gospel. Here's my small effort at turning us to you because of what you did, what you didn't do, and what Jesus said about you.

Thank you for the days and labor—whatever that toil—you spent so that you could give Jesus that memorable gift.

Thank you for your example of unwavering stability in the circle of ministry that was as rewarding as it was painful, as quiet as it was bold, and as full of preparation as it was power.

Thank you for not allowing the people who spoke poorly of you to change your mind about seeing Jesus, anointing Jesus, reaching Jesus, and preparing Jesus.

Thank you for the courage you had to walk into a room with some who didn't know you as a gift and an evangelist, who didn't know you as the primer of all our best sermons about the resurrected One.

Thank you for the resilience you possessed in your interiority that allowed you to hear what was said about you by people who really never saw you and allowed you to brace yourself in the company of the Teacher who would die to prove how valuable you were.

Thank you for your days of being brutalized by unkind others, of being told you were dispensable, of being talked down to even though you were in a class by yourself—esteemed by Jesus to have a place no one else would.

Thank you for your place in the cloud of witnesses, in that collected humble wisdom tradition, there among sister giants whose records go un-examined because you are women.

Thank you for the stamina you've had in eternity while listening to the good news preached, listening for your name to be mentioned, though the gospel writers in the centuries since didn't keep it.

Thank you for waiting in heavenly space for our broken imaginations to attempt to name you well even while we attempted to state things about Jesus whom you loved, held, and cared for in that inestimable, physical way.

Thank you for being so important to Jesus that he said we'd mention you whenever we mentioned him and for the impact you made that moved him to include you in such a close way to any mentioning of God's displayed work.

Thank you for waiting.

May you and others like you never be forgotten. May you never be a footnote. May you share the eternal stage with him who sits upon an enduring throne.

Guiding Questions

1. Who comes to mind as a person who should be included in proclamations about Jesus?
2. What ways can you acknowledge the gifts of others in your discipleship?
3. How have others helped you worship God?

One Next Step

Take a step to remember the un-named and usually unmentioned people in your life. Think back to your way of coming to faith. Who participated in that process? The names of those people are worth lifting, hearing, and blessing. If you are still able to contact them, check in with them. Update them on your faith, your journey, and your ways of being with God. Try to find one simple way of thanking them. Incorporate them into the collective wisdom that this unnamed woman from Mark's gospel participates in.

Prayer

I have not been as thankful as I can be. Make me thankful. Turn me into a person of praise. Grant me the ability to praise you and to compliment others. Use me to be a person of gratitude and wonder. Sensitize my inside so that I am more thankful than before. And I will praise you. Amen.

Blessing

There are wise ones from before, wise people from times prior. I will make effort to remember them and honor them as I remember Jesus.

Yes, You Are the One

In the evening Jesus arrived with the Twelve. As they were at the table eating, Jesus said, "I tell you the truth, one of you eating with me here will betray me. Greatly distressed, each one asked in turn, "Am I the one?" (Mark 14:17-19, NLT)

When Christians do things wrong, their faith becomes a target. Think back to stories in the media or to anecdotes that you've heard when a Christian or a person of faith committed a terrible act. You'll probably remember their faith being brought into the mix. You've heard and I've heard many times something along the lines of "Christians don't do that." Or, "And, he calls himself a person of faith." Or, some other specific and routine identification of terrible behavior with a specific religious group. This has happened a lot in our country with Muslims in recent years.

It's easy to take one characteristic of a person or one behavior from a person and make them that characteristic, fix them as that behavior. That's where labels come from and stereotypes too.

This passage lifts a nerve-racking dynamic. People of faith actually need their faith to be better. This passage and the rest of them in the Bible assume that people need what's in those pages. In other words, the practices of your faith make a difference in your life. Think of it. You being at the table with Jesus—with your background and your past—makes you eligible for being identified as a betrayer *and* as a follower.

The scripture doesn't pull your behavior away from you. It doesn't dismiss the future act of betraying. Jesus actually warns the group. "One of you eating with me here will betray me." That underlines the behavior. It tells you that Jesus saw it as worth mentioning. What the scripture story always underlines is that person's inclusion in the eating community. Judas was there. Judas wasn't excused. Judas wasn't ineligible. Judas was a betrayer and a follower.

The disciples knew at a fundamental level that they were capable of harming Jesus, turning on him, and mistreating him. Looking to each other, they all questioned their ability to do what only one of them would. This was an expression of deep humility. In that room, at that table, bread and wine in hand, they all knew that they were as close to love as they were to fear, as close to loyalty as they were to betrayal.

They saw within their fields of vision the ability to defend Jesus and to defame him. Judas ended up the one who acted but not because he was the only one who could've done so. All of the twelve sat at that table. All of them heard Jesus open with that ambiguous and troubling comment. They each needed their faith, and they needed it to save them from themselves.

Faith for them would be the means for wholeness. Each person at the table with Jesus would need faith in Jesus to minister to the parts of them they were true and powerful and contrary. Keep the contrary part in view. It's the contrary, dark, even dismal parts of yourself that are hard to view, and almost impossible to accept. Acceptance doesn't mean agreement. It doesn't mean unexamined. It means understanding what belongs.

If you are a betraying Judas or a betraying John, what do you gain by ignoring that? You gain nothing by rolling your eyes at Jesus. You gain a new perspective about yourself, though, if you hear him, take him seriously, and begin the slow soul-work of asking good questions like, "Am I the one?"

Guiding Questions

1. What occurred to you about yourself as you read this reflection?
2. How have you felt judged for your dark, sinful, and challenging sides?
3. How has God given you grace for those same sides?

One Next Step

Take a step to notice your flaws. Spend a minute thinking through the sides and parts of you that you aren't excited about. Perhaps there is one side that you are ashamed of or one that you don't talk about. Sit with that part. Get curious about it. See if there is a story about where that part of you came from or about that part's future. You might notice where that part of you fits with the rest of yourself. You might notice a large distance between it and who you usually consider yourself to be. This step is about noticing *that* part. Notice it and you're already closer to accepting it.

Prayer

Grant me the patience to see myself fully.
Help me be gracious especially when I see my darkness.
Make me gentle with the parts of me that aren't public.
I am not proud of myself all the time.
When I betray you, teach me unconditional love.
So that in my living, I become a lover like you.
Amen.

Blessing

I am not just what people see. I am more. I am more.

Next Steps

This list is a collection of the "One Next Step" sections from each reflection. I offer them as a list so that you can return to it as you continue to follow and be in step with Jesus. Use it however it seems wise.

1. Notice God's prophets.
2. Consider John's message, whatever it is.
3. Ritualize your discipleship.
4. Go out among the animals.
5. Summarize the gospel in your own words.
6. Invite someone to join you in following Jesus.
7. Consider your limits.
8. Step toward healing by examining a part of your soul that's been bruised.
9. Plan a beginning.
10. Wait by intentionally sitting with what's present.
11. Ask the Holy Spirit to empower you to choose differently.
12. Turn your ear (or your inner ear) to what Jesus is saying to you now.
13. Consider how you can accept a person you're currently struggling to accept.
14. Take an inventory of your company.

15. Take a risk by doing something consistent with your faith but that you've never done.
16. Recall a painful time from your past and sit with that pain in the company of Jesus.
17. Draw your spiritual family tree.
18. Consider your dark places, places where God is working but you don't know how.
19. Write a prayer for someone who needs God's gift.
20. Consider feedback you've heard recently.
21. Put yourself in a position where you have to wait.
22. Make a list of the things and places your energy and attention go.
23. Answer Jesus' question: why are you so afraid?
24. Offer someone a blessing.
25. Notice daily where you've spoken about your spiritual life and where you haven't.
26. Take Jesus on a tour of your neighborhood.
27. Choose one part of your story and think it through.
28. Expose people to a thing God did, a thing God said, or a gift God gave you.
29. Investigate the stories of others who have left to follow.
30. Bow your head when you hear of the death of someone.
31. Study your fears.

32. Sit down with someone you disagree with to talk about the scriptures.
33. Express gratitude to God for who you are and how God has made you.
34. Claim a healing.
35. Review your day.
36. Notice the impact of words on your life.
37. Hold onto one word or phrase from Jesus this week.
38. Take a class about something that'll help you grow.
39. Have a conversation with a friend you haven't seen in a while.
40. Consider who you've left and what you've lost.
41. Sit next to the suffering in your life.
42. Train one of your desires to be in step with Jesus.
43. Turn your wants toward God by serving.
44. Tell yourself that you walk in step with Jesus.
45. Be vulnerable considering your disappointments with God.
46. Make a list of when you've felt far from Jesus.
47. Write a list of changes you know you need to make but that you've resisted.
48. Consider the readying reminders of death that Jesus has provided.
49. Name the un-named, usually unmentioned people in your life who have led you well.

50. Try to notice your flaws.

www.ingramcontent.com/pod-product-compliance
Lightning Source LLC
LaVergne TN
LVHW041614070426
835507LV00008B/230